Behaving as
US

The Art of Cooperation

By Kenneth E. Scherr

"There are two kinds of people in the world: those who divide the world into two kinds of people and those who don't."

- Robert Benchley

Copyright Page

First paperback edition.

ISBN: 979-8-9872166-0-6 (paperback)
ISBN: 979-8-9872166-1-3 (e-book)

Library of Congress Control Number: 2022921354

Published by Scherr Publishing
www.scherrpublishing.com
info@scherrpublishing.com

Dedication Page

To everyone wishing for peace.

Table of Contents

Preface

It was 2020 when I received my ballot in the mail. At last, now that I was of age, I could do my civic duty and vote in the presidential election. I was thrilled that I could finally voice my opinion and take part in the democratic process, something that has only been possible relatively recently in human history.

Just like every American who decided to vote in the 2020 election, I was faced with 2 dominant choices: Trump or Biden. Yes, I could have filled in the blank or voted third party, but to keep things simple, these two candidates were the focus of the campaign season and the talk of the town, or better yet, the world. To me, this was a big decision, and a tough decision. I wanted to make what I felt like was "the right choice."

During the campaign season, I heard non-stop opinions and rhetoric on social media and the news both in support and disapproval of the candidates. Flooded with information, I wanted to take a step back, do some digging around myself, and make my own decision, uninfluenced by what media pundits or YouTube channels had to say. From what I had heard in the news, both seemed terrible in some respects, and both had upsides in others. Depending on which outlet or personality I listened to, they had drastically different opinions of the candidates and were all extremely passionate about their opinions. I did not know who was right or what authoritative source had my best interests in mind. For all I knew, everyone could be equally as right as they were wrong, so I did not want to believe 100% of what anyone said and would take everything with a grain of salt. I remember thinking to myself, "I want this vote to reflect 'me,' whatever that means." I did not want to vote for someone just because my friends were voting for them or because they were the candidate my favorite news station propped up.

I remember the night I told my friends I did not know who I was going to vote for, and that I was starting to lean toward one candidate over the other. Their facial expressions twisted with dissatisfaction and disgust, as though something with a foul stench caught their senses. This was not only because I was uncertain, but because I was slightly leaning toward "the other guy."

My friend, their name omitted, was confused and angry, in a way, at me that I was not on board with who he thought was the better choice. "It's so obvious," they might have said, "you have to vote for my guy to save the country," or some classic sensationalizing to that effect. Now, I don't care if that comes from someone on the left, right, or anywhere else on the spectrum—statements like that are engulfed in bias.

Thankfully, this political disagreement did not stain our friendships, though I have now experienced opinions tampering with what seemed at the time like good relationships. Like mature adults, from then on, my friends and I would talk more about politics and things of the sort when we would hang out by the fire, never getting too bent out of shape by what anyone had to say. At the end of the day, we were all best friends, and no opinion, whether jocular or serious, could permeate our bonds. These conversations would not always stay the politest, and vulgar names were occasionally flung at each other. But when you are with friends, you can risk calling them a few names. After all, you love them, and they love you; they should accept you for your opinions if they are truly your friend, and you theirs. Still, though sometimes it may have gotten heated and provocative, it was, overall, a great way to learn more about each other and to practice tolerating different views, perspective taking, and other complex social skills.

Although we had disagreements about who might be a better candidate or which policy decision is best, it was incredibly beneficial for us to talk through our disagreements and learn about each other. We embraced the free flow of information and honest self-expression. Even if we did not change the others' beliefs, it was a perfect way to at least challenge everyone's beliefs respectfully and get everyone thinking critically. This is of mutual benefit.

I have chosen to open the introduction with this short story about the 2020 presidential election and my friends to acquaint the reader with the focus of this book. There could have been many ways to start this introduction, but I see this as the most personal and relatable. As with any endeavor, academic or entrepreneurial, if one chooses to wait to find the perfect way to start, then one will forever be waiting. Sometimes, it is best to just take the leap and then later accept the judgments of peers and the market. Therefore, I welcome, value, respect, and most of all, appreciate honest comments and critiques of my work, and I interpret all perspectives as helpful.

My story serves as a model of the kinds of behavior I want my readers to incorporate into their daily lives. And given that this book begins with such a story, I see it as only right that I end the book with a similar, but much more in-depth, story to really drive the point home. I intend for the last chapter, "The Story of Daryl Davis," to be the spaghetti that sticks. The behavior I intend to model for the reader is as follows: *the maturity to listen to and respect others, the appreciation of new perspectives, the importance of honest self-expression, education, and courage.* It is my goal to motivate the reader to use this underappreciated set of skills more. In politics and beyond, the lessons described in this book are appropriate for all complex social situations in which those involved intend to maintain peace and productivity.

Unfortunately, there is a growing minority of the country that does not have the luck that my friends and I possess hanging in my backyard sitting by the fire or, as you will see, the skills of Daryl Davis. For these folks, the probability of enacting such behavior in a legitimate situation is unlikely. The likelihood that they will be cooperative is not too strong. Some people do not demonstrate the skills of **cooperation** listed in the preceding paragraph, and this is a deficit that affects the country in its entirety. This is not to say that these people have not learned these skills but rather that they have not reliably come to exert a conditioned response. In simpler terms, this means they may know what this prosocial behavior looks like but hardly ever exhibit such behavior in a real-life situation. They can describe it or even act it out when asked in a controlled setting but struggle to behave properly when it's the "real deal." Sometimes they do, but much of the time, they do not. Thus, I intend this book to be the stimulus that motivates the prosocial/cooperative behaviors listed above in the growing minority and the culture at large.

People in this growing minority can become "triggered," the common colloquial phrase for being agitated or distressed by the opinions of others. This inability to handle the speech of others with emotional maturity is a growing problem that I will address in this book. Being able to tolerate the opinions of others in a mature conversation is at the heart of cooperation and a functioning culture. This doesn't even consider the overall emotional health of the triggered, and for that matter *all*, individuals. It is my intent to help the reader develop emotional intelligence. This stressful response to the opinions of others — being triggered — is something I intend to use this book to help alleviate by giving model examples of emotionally intelligent and mature behavior.

Moreover, I will address some underlying problems hindering cooperation with which all humans are cursed. Though it is, for the most part, a gift of evolution, one of these problems is the automatic association between previously neutral stimuli, otherwise known as classical conditioning. Specifically, in the context of this book, this is the conditioning, or learning, of the disgust reflex in response to "them," which is a way I refer to those who are the out-group or the "other." "They" are those whose very opinions are "triggering." This learned response of disgust to those of an opposing persuasion, "them," is a core issue I seek to address and help resolve. In this conversation on learning and conditioning, I will also discuss other forms of learning, such as operant conditioning, and will just slightly dip my toes into the aspects of language involved in this whole kerfuffle.

In setting out to accomplish the difficult goals I have just laid forth, I begin in Chapter One by introducing the reader to the old, or perhaps ancient, philosophies that were, at the time, the greatest attempts on written record to understand human behavior. Then, after following the trail of great thought leaders, in Chapter Two, I introduce a modern philosophy of behavior dubbed radical behaviorism by American psychologist B. F. Skinner. I use the content in the first two chapters to focus the reader's attention on the idea that behavior is being further and more completely explained by analyzing biology and the environment as opposed to the idea of free will. I chose to structure the book in this fashion to (a) properly introduce the science of behavior and (b) discuss the lack of free will that radical behaviorism implies and how this relates to cooperation. It has been this history and new philosophy that have contributed to my motivation to listen to others with maturity and respect, appreciate new perspectives, value honest self-expression, education, and courage. Thus, I only see it as right to prime the reader with the same understanding so that they can best interpret my message.

Chapter Three details the vocabulary and behavioral concepts that are used to describe and explain the reasons for behavior, which then leads to the discussion in Chapter Four about the implications of a lack of free will, which this philosophy of the science of behavior entails. I see this chapter as possibly the most controversial of all, not because of the legitimacy of the opinion but because it is a hard thing to hear for most people, who hold the idea of an inner determinism close to their heart. For that reason, I begin the chapter with an extension of Chapter Three and discuss choice behavior to maintain the continuity of the explanation of complex behaviors. All of this in Part One functions to lay a ground for the reader to properly digest the contents of Part Two. There, in Chapter Five, I go over the problem of "us/them" behavior (or in-group/out-group behavior), its divisive origins, the first step in solving this problem, and the further problems that are to be addressed after the first step. In Chapters Six and Seven, I dive into the solutions to the remaining troubles that were not addressed in Chapter 6. Finally, as I have already mentioned, in Chapter 8, I conclude the book with the exemplar of model behavior I want the reader to imitate: the story of Daryl Davis. Not only is it a story I will be telling my future children to teach them these life skills, but I see it as an underappreciated parable that needs to be spread more thoroughly throughout the culture.

As stated earlier in this introduction, if I were to wait until I devised "the perfect chapter scheme," I would never have started writing, for there are always improvements to be made. This is a motto I have kept with me in writing this book, and I hope it rubs off some on the reader. It reflects my deepest values: education and courage. I recognize that no matter how well-read I am, there will always be more to know, and I will not always be correct—the articulation of nature could always be deeper. But that is the beauty in valuing education and courage; failure is another learning opportunity which creates new goals to work toward in parallel with the valorization of education.

Part One:
Foundation

Chapter I

The Old Philosophy

"Mistakes are merely steps up the ladder." (1)
— Paul Meyer

....

Consciousness, the conceptual self, and complex behaviors are enigmatic phenomena that philosophy and science have historically struggled to grapple with. It is to nobody's surprise that a fair number of past assumptions have been wrong. I use the quote that begins this chapter and say this to emphasize the point that I first iterated in the introduction: there is always more to learn. The articulation of nature can always be better than it currently is. This simply means that we have been wrong about a great deal, we are wrong about much currently, and we will continue to learn from our wrongs and set a course for committing new wrongs. The point is, however, that even with a history of mistakes and misjudgments, we continue to grow and fulfill the value of education. To do this, though, to move on from preceding beliefs and have a change of heart, so to speak, is a courageous task and therefore not an easy task. Thus, it is my goal to make this courageous choice an easier choice, using this history lesson to help visualize a different perspective — a new outlook that can make the reader more understanding and accepting of their own limitations. It is my presumption that with every history lesson comes a lesson in humility, and this will be no exception.

In this chapter, I will first give an overview of the conceptual understanding of behavior throughout history, from Aristotle to Freud. This is an introductory walkthrough, and I will happily admit that it is a very brief and limited one at that. The history of the philosophy and science of behavior will be used here to set the stage for the reader in two important ways. First, it will establish an introductory level of understanding the human condition through a historical lens. This will allow us to see where human thought was heading in the right direction and where we were embarrassingly wrong. Second, it is meant to establish a frame of reference for the rest of the book, a sense of intellectual humility that — putting pride aside — will prompt the interpretation I intend.

To understand the significance of where we are today, we must appreciate the mistakes of yesterday. We begin to appreciate the little things the more we realize just how big they truly are. For instance, the running water in your house, the microwave in your kitchen, the cellphone, and the internet are modern inventions that we all too often take for granted. It might be hard to appreciate the technology of central cooling air, for example, but when you live in a hot city such as Las Vegas during the summer, if that AC breaks, you begin to have a new respect for the protection that technology has provided. I am speaking from experience. Being aware of how far we have come can put into perspective how far we can still reach.

First, it is important to recognize that psychology is a science that diverged from the art of philosophy only about 150 years ago. Because of this and many psychologists in the field doing a terrible job of explaining their viewpoints to the public, many of the philosophical roots of psychology still haunt the field today and the public's view of psychology and behavior. So, to start fixing the wrongs that my predecessors have laid, I will do a brief dive into history, looking back at the leading philosophers of consciousness and questioning their rationales. I do this not only to doublecheck their claims but also to make certain we have not wrongfully assumed the totality of knowledge about behavior (spoilers: we haven't!). After pointing out fallacies of historical reasoning and understanding that logic, we can then learn lessons from these past perceptions or mistakes and formulate new conceptions. Having a brief understanding of the philosophical history of consciousness allows us to deconstruct our ignorant restriction of possibilities and start to consider new articulations.

A Brief Look at History

I will start this lesson with the Greek philosopher Aristotle (384–322 B.C.E.). Let the reader note that I will skip over many notable names, and this is not a complete history — for a more complete history, I recommend reading the two volume series *The Scientific Evolution of Psychology* by J.R. Kantor. To begin with, Aristotle believed that humans possessed what he called a "rational soul," which he claimed resided in the heart. Now, with today's knowledge, I know it may seem strange to imagine that behavior originates from the heart, but keep in mind the concept of intellectual humility that I have frequently mentioned. Aristotle is one of the greatest minds to ever live, yet even he was still prone to mistakes. This rational soul, Aristotle describes, is the source of human intellect and requires some perceptual mechanisms, such as the brain, to function. In other words, this intellect provides the organism with the ability to interpret the world and make calculated choices, biologically equipping it to categorize nature and solve problems. Thus, in Aristotle, a "soul," which delegates behavior, requires a physical body. This dualistic approach to behavior, in which the soul requires but is also distinct from the material substrate, is one that I will revisit down the road with later historical figures. Aside from this dualism his work makes abundantly clear, Aristotle's psychology is a branch of biology (2). With this emphasis on biology, he produced the momentum for further investigation into understanding the mind and behavior from a scientific perspective (3). For the reader, and humanity, the journey to understand behavior is on its way.

    Though Aristotle is a household name, this does not mean that all of his propositions were correct, as I have already mentioned. There is no need to worship the ground he stands on, as if he were a prophet. Though groundbreaking for his time, his thoughts are incompatible with what we know today. Even children might laugh at the idea that the heart is responsible for thought—the fact that the brain is more responsible than the heart for thinking is trivial today. This goes to show that, just like the technology of central air, it is easy to take for granted the knowledge and technology of today. Nonetheless, his achievements were momentous for his time, and they still influence the scholars of the present. However, the biggest takeaway from his work—at least in the context of this book—is the emergence of the idea that there is something inside the person that is the reason why the person behaves as they do. Though he deemed this the "soul," he nonetheless recognized that biology was fundamental in understanding why organisms behave as they do. Whether this be an early allusion to genes or a metaphysical entity pulling the strings, it is a recognition that there is something important going on internally. Still, although he was wrong about the heart being the focal point, he was on the right track in recognizing that there are things inside of the body that facilitate behavior and that there are natural constraints on and allowances of behavior based on biology and physics.

After the Earth takes a few victory laps around the sun, then comes Claudius Galenus (Galen, 130–210 A.D.), an experienced physician by trade. Galen created a new theory based on the works of Hippocrates, Plato, Socrates, and Aristotle combined. Galen believed in a material tripartite soul, or three distinct souls with distinct functions and anatomical locations: the liver as the appetitive soul, the heart as the spiritual soul, and the brain as the rational soul. Galen also laid the groundwork for the idea of the subconscious by postulating that the mental and physical were intimately intertwined, with no distinction. He thought that some parts of the soul did not function by awareness or rationalization—that the organism does things without "realizing" that it is doing so.

However, the organism also has certain functions that operate under conscious awareness. Yet, even though he believed each soul to be intertwined with an anatomy, he still believed in an immortal soul, something separate from the physical—again, a separation of the physical and the mental. Still, besides his belief in an immortal soul (which is a mentalistic approach), he contributed a mechanistic approach to the notion that different organs perform different functions—another insight that is widely taken for granted today (4).

With Galen, we see a breakthrough—specifically, that organisms do things without thought or below conscious awareness. This is the realization of what I will later call "contingencies of survival," or things that organisms have learned to do due to belonging to a species that has evolved unique (and shared) traits. Cell repair, digestion, and pumping blood are all operations that the organism performs, not because it "chooses to" (choice and free will being a topic later in the book) but "because of" natural selection. I say "because of" (in quotes) since assigning behavioral causality simply to an evolutionary mechanism is a premature explanation for behavior, and there is more to the puzzle than just evolutionary biology. This means that even if an organism is predisposed to certain behaviors because of its biology, the organism will still behave relative to its context— but more on this later.[1]

---

[1] This alludes to the second major feature of radical behaviorism, which is the nurture aspect of behavior, or the environmentally specific, operant conditioning sense of contingencies of reinforcement.

Then, after about 1,400 head-spinning years of Earth flying through the galaxy, René Descartes emerges in France (1596–1650). Echoing the mechanistic approach held by Galen, Descartes operated under the belief that nature functions like a machine. Recalling Galen's notion that some parts of the soul — or behaviors, to say it more precisely — operate without awareness, Descartes emphasized preprogrammed motor responses or reflexes, which are responses that occur quickly in response to a sharp stimulus. Rather than positing a soul behind behavior, he described that an external stimulus from the environment causes events to occur in the nervous system that result in predetermined responses. No director of action needs to be in charge; no soul is necessary (5). However, even after recognizing that some responses of the organism (reflexes) transpire in direct response to the environment and are biologically predetermined, Descartes still struggled with the idea of free will and ultimately gave in to mind/body dualism, or the idea of a mechanical body with an immaterial cognitive machine — also like Galen.

Looking back at this point in history, with Descartes' shortcomings, I think to myself — finally! We have the long overdue approach stating that responses of the organism happen because of something other than a soul! (This is not to say that a soul does not exist, per se, but just that even if there is a soul, it is not responsible for, or the cause of, behavior and consciousness). This pivot in philosophy starts to bring us closer to a more complete explanation of behavior, one that recognizes the impact of both the organism's biology AND its environment. I say pivot because it is not a complete step in another direction but rather a setup to pass the ball to his successors. This "pivot" is evident in his failure to extend his notion of reflexes and contextual responses to the rest of behavior;[2] he had a groundbreaking idea but failed to run with it all the way. This hesitancy to attribute all responses of the organism to biological-environmental relations (what is called nature and nurture) and the reference instead to a soul or some inner self guiding free will (which I will discuss later) is a common shortcoming when trying to analyze behavior, which we still see today.[3]

After some more time jetting through the cosmos, in the 1640s, an entirely opposed worldview was introduced by physicist Thomas Hobbes of England, who rejected Descartes' notion of an immaterial soul. Hobbes saw the body functioning as a material machine, with no room for mysticism or ghosts. He adopted an engineering mentality and thought that consciousness was another physical part of the machine that is the human body. This method of analysis passed on to his assistant, William Petty, who also argued that the body was an assembly of parts that ran like a machine (7). Both Hobbes and Petty were deeply mechanistic, more so than Descartes or Galen. Unlike Descartes, it was because of his history of being an exceptional anatomist that Petty could not ignore the brain as a central factor when analyzing behavior and consciousness.

Descartes, with his pivot, passed the ball to Hobbes to expand on the mechanistic point of view

---

[2] "Response of the organism" and "behavior" are synonyms in this book.

[3] I will show why this is so when I further explain what radical behaviorism is.

that there are reasons for behavior other than a soul. Hobbes was able to develop the idea that the body functions like a machine in that each part of the organism has a purpose in the function of that organism, ultimately bringing us one step closer to a more complete analysis of how organisms operate. Yet, Hobbes still did not nail down behavior and consciousness, as he thought that consciousness existed somewhere in the body as a part of the organism, making him partly responsible for copy theory, or the idea that images, perceptions, memories, and so on are literally stored in one's brain (a claim refuted by radical behaviorism). This way of thinking is still pervasive today, with people believing that memories are actually *things* that exist in someone's brain and can be *retrieved* at a later date when commanded. The hard truth is that we can look for consciousness as a part of the brain, and we have surely done so, but we will never be successful. If we look for memories or behaviors inside the brain, they will never be found. Behavior, consciousness, and memory are verbs or actions, not nouns representing objects that can be found in nature (8).

After a few more advances by the successors of Hobbes, the world was ready for the entrance of John Locke, a British empiricist (1632–1734). Locke famously introduced the idea of the *tabula rasa,* or blank slate, in 1689 as a way to describe how the mind is formed only from experience and self-reflection, an idea that continued the debate on "nature versus nurture" (9). This debate, for those readers not familiar with it, is the argument over whether behavior is better explained by the biology of the individual or environmental conditions. Now, for the most part, there is no longer a debate between *either* nature *or* nurture, as it is recognized that both play integral roles in the production of an individual's behavior. Thus, the idea of a blank slate is overly simple and incorrect. It claims that the organism's behavior and conscious experiences are completely molded by experience and not at all by biology. This gives us yet another example of even the greatest minds being wrong.

Locke's idea of *tabula rasa* took a major step in the right direction by recognizing that the environment has more of an impact on behavior and consciousness than Descartes, or anyone else, had originally thought (again, Descartes thought the only connections between the environment and behavior were 1:1 responses called reflexes and did not believe the environment had any other control over behavior, as he gave into the belief in free will). However, his overemphasis on the environmental impact and underestimation of the starting place of the organism led some people to emphasize, too heavily, the impact of the environment on behavior. Though all behavior is *context-specific*, the environment is still only half of the equation. Such an overemphasis on the environmental impact on behavior is the biggest critique those in other disciplines have of behaviorists (which, to me, shows that they simply do not understand *radical* behaviorism, which can partly be due to stains of the past). Even academic superstars, such as Robert Sapolsky (a neuroscientist and primatologist) at Stanford, critique behaviorism for claims that overemphasize the impact of the environment on behavior. Citing John Watson, Sapolsky said the following:

> Give me a dozen healthy infants, well-formed, and my own specified world to bring them up in and I'll guarantee to take any one at random

and train him to become any type of specialist I might select—doctor, lawyer, artist, merchant-chief and, yes, even beggar-man and thief, regardless of his talents, penchants, tendencies, abilities, vocations, and race of his ancestors. *(10)*

I can and do acknowledge that bold claims such as this are far-fetched and are precisely why some people have a poor perception of what behaviorism is. However, do not be fooled; this is not the full quote (how fun, a twist!). Sapolsky, as well as most people who cite this quote, leave out the very next sentence, in which Watson admits that he is making this claim in jest. The full quote finishes by saying, "I am going beyond my facts and I admit it, but so have the advocates of the contrary and they have been doing it for many thousands of years" (11). Watson recognizes that he is making an exaggerated claim but does so while acknowledging that it has always been done. (This is a point that Sapolsky would be pleasantly surprised to learn about and that he would agree with. This idea of those in their field overemphasizing their fields' impact or importance on behavior is precisely a point of his 2018 book *Behave*).

Now, we focus our attention on David Hume (1711– 1776), a Scottish philosopher who returned to Hobbes' and Petty's more mechanistic line of argument and asserted that the prior notions of a supernatural soul were delusional. Hume countered Descartes' dualist approach by reasoning that *all* events had cause-and-effect relationships rather than just 1:1 reflexes (the only leeway on environmental interaction that Descartes gave to consciousness and behavior). Hume concluded that "all reasonings concerning matters of fact seem to be founded on the relation of Cause and Effect" (12). Causality, for Hume, relies on proximity in time and space and a necessary connection that distinguishes itself from mere correlation. By acknowledging that correlation is not causation, Hume set the stage for studying behavior as a science: behaviorism. Hume, however, was not a behaviorist, as behaviorism still would not be founded until after Hume died.

What I said about Descartes' observation regarding reflexes as behaviors in relation to the environment, I will say about Hume's expansion on that notion, even though he was still not completely correct. Although he was narrowly focused on proximity in time and space (which, to be sure, are incredibly important elements, but not the only factors for analysis), he realized that there is more to behavior than reflexes and that there must be a material explanation for everything. We are getting closer to an explanation of behavior (and consciousness) that can account not for free will and an immaterial soul that is outside the reach of science but a mix of biological and environmental interaction! This nature–nurture entanglement is at the heart of radical behaviorism, but more on that later.

Before continuing to explicate this idea of behavior being a result of events' proximity in time and space, I want to acknowledge Englishman Charles Darwin (1809–1882) and his impact on radical behaviorism and the work of B.F. Skinner. Darwin argued against the mind/body dualism approach taken by predecessors such as Aristotle, Galen, and Descartes, and was the first to bring an evolutionary approach to the conversation on consciousness and the selection of behavior.

Darwin argued that humans and other animals all experienced what is called consciousness but on different levels. He concluded that "the difference in mind between man and the higher animals, great as it is, certainly is one of degree and not of kind" (13). In other words, through evolution, all animals are capable of consciousness, but the human species has developed a unique form of consciousness. Darwin further concludes that if man can experience perception, it must have been selected during the long process of the evolution through natural selection of traits that promise a greater chance of survival (in radical behaviorist terms, selection by "contingencies of survival").

Darwin progressed the field in a very important way by arguing that other animals are conscious and that consciousness is not an experience unique to humans bestowed upon us by the divine. As you might expect, the theory of evolution had major scientific impacts and faced equally significant societal pushback. Like many other ideas that, historically, move away from explaining behavior by a soul and free will but instead invoke factors that are seemingly out of the individual's control, Darwin received his expected criticisms. Still, after all the dust has settled, his theory has been triumphant and is now taken for granted. This was a major stride in the explanation of behavior and support for the idea that organisms develop and behave specific to their environmental context.

Before moving on, however, I want to clarify Darwin's theory so that the reader is not left confused (as I will reference it quite a bit in the following chapter). *Selection* is a *process* in which those already exhibiting certain features *are more likely to* survive, prevail, and most importantly, reproduce. Environmental conditions during the evolutionary history of a species determine which characteristics prevail in that species. The key takeaway from this is that *it is the environment that selects the particular feature and not the organism itself, somehow isolated from the forces of the environment and biology.* Simply put, the species had no input on the matter (an idea that I will focus on in radical behaviorism in the context of free will and why organisms behave as they do).

Now that we have covered Darwin and his theory *explaining the origins and evolution of* consciousness (though not exactly what consciousness is, however) as a product of contingencies of survival, we can continue down the list of those who expanded on the idea that environmental factors are the causes of behavior rather than an internal— immaterial and metaphysically separate—soul.

Like many great innovations, the next development happened by accident. In comes Russian scientist Ivan Pavlov (1849–1936). I say his discovery was by accident because he was conducting research on the digestion of dogs and very focused on physiology rather than psychology when he noticed that the dogs' physical reactions to food subtly changed over time (i.e., the dogs' reflexive salivation in response to food). He did not expect this to happen or list it anywhere in his experiment, but it was so interesting that he kept track of it anyway. At first, the dogs would only salivate when the food was placed in front of them. However, later, the dogs salivated slightly before their food arrived. Pavlov brilliantly realized that they were salivating at the noises that were consistently present before the food arrived— specifically, the sound of a food cart approaching.

To test his hypothesis (remember, this observation had nothing to do with his current research), Pavlov set up an experiment in which he rang a bell shortly before presenting food to the dogs. At first, the dogs exhibited no response to the bells. Eventually, the dogs began to salivate at the sound of the bell alone! (14) This was a learned reflex. This transformation of stimulus control and learning from pairing things in space and time is known as *respondent conditioning* (or, properly dedicated to Pavlov, as Pavlovian conditioning or classical conditioning). This kind of conditioning expands on the idea of Descartes, who, as the reader can recall, proposed 1:1 reflexes. Pavlov, by showing that there can be, in fact, more than one stimulus that can elicit the same reflex, and that those other stimuli that elicit the response can be learned during the course of an animal's lifetime, revamped the idea of Descartes' strict 1:1 reflex theory. Science is making progress!

Now, to better understand respondent conditioning, it is essential to understand the following key terms. The first two terms are *unconditioned stimulus* and *unconditioned response*. For starters, anything 'unconditioned' is something unlearned. These are basic biological responses that an animal is born able to perform without training. The organism is *biologically predisposed* to behave in certain ways in certain environments, given its evolutionary history or *contingencies of survival* (this is precisely why I wanted to squeeze Darwin in where I did). For example, in Pavlov's experiment, the dog salivating at the taste of food was an unconditioned response, and the food was an unconditioned stimulus. The dog did not have to learn to salivate when food was placed in its mouth; it just did.

The next term is *neutral stimulus*. This is something in the environment with which the animal has no established relationship, so it elicits no response. For example, in Pavlov's experiment, the bell was originally a neutral stimulus because, upon the first encounter with the bell, the dog did not salivate or behave in any way in response to the bell. It is not until the bell is paired over multiple trials with the presentation of food that the bell takes on some role in causing, or eliciting, salivation.

This is a perfect way to introduce *conditioned stimuli* and *conditioned responses*. In opposition to "unconditioned," that anything is "conditioned" means that it is something that has been learned over the animal's lifetime. For example, in Pavlov's experiment, the dog learning to salivate at the sound of the bell is a conditioned response that then becomes a conditioned stimulus. Thus, a neutral stimulus becomes a conditioned stimulus by repeatedly being paired with unconditioned and already conditioned stimuli.

Notice how the unconditioned response and the conditioned response are the same (salivation) but are elicited by different environmental stimuli. This is precisely where the idea of 1:1 interaction (proposed by Descartes) falls apart. In the example of Pavlov's experiment, the dog developed a 2:1 stimulus-response pattern. Because there is no limit on the number of conditioned stimuli that can come to elicit each reflex, the exact number of conditioned stimuli is specific to the individual.

Overall, Pavlov's experiments began to draw scientists' attention to *automatic processes* in the body that occur without "choice" or effortful awareness. This brings the science of behavior and

the philosophy of that science one step closer to a
more complete understanding of behavior.

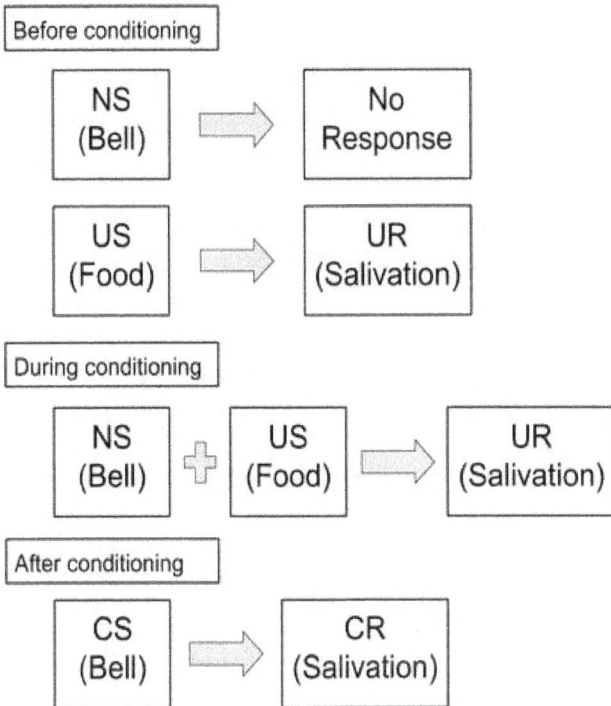

Before conditioning

| NS (Bell) | ⟹ | No Response |

| US (Food) | ⟹ | UR (Salivation) |

During conditioning

| NS (Bell) | ✚ | US (Food) | ⟹ | UR (Salivation) |

After conditioning

| CS (Bell) | ⟹ | CR (Salivation) |

During the same lifespan as Pavlov, there then
entered a German scientist who discussed the idea
of the *unconscious* and took a deeper look into the
automatic and context-specific processes that occur
below conscious awareness. This is Sigmund Freud
(1856–1939). His clinical approach, revolutionary at
the time but now outdated, was called
psychoanalysis, and it took the world by storm
(though mostly after his death). Freud created an
elaborate theory of the unconscious and went on to
develop a model of a "psychic structure"
comprising the id, ego, and superego.

Each aspect of the psyche has its own respective function. Freud postulated that certain drives (i.e., the libido and aggression) and anxieties (i.e., neurotic, moral, realistic) motivate behavior (15). And though much of Freud's work and reputation have been tainted by his cocaine use and the famous Oedipus complex, he nevertheless laid the foundation for scientific research to uncover the inner workings of the unconscious. As acknowledged by his successor, B.F. Skinner, who will be the focus of the next chapter, Freud's "great achievement, was to apply to principle of cause and effect to human behavior. Aspects of behavior which had hitherto been regarded as whimsical, aimless, or accidental, Freud traced to relevant variables"(16).

Freud is deserving of all the tomatoes you can throw at him, but so is everyone. It is important, however, to ensure that the achievements of his work are still recognized and remembered. It would be a shame if we took his work, and the research that came from it, for granted, yet I can already foresee that unfortunate situation. In almost every psychology class I took during my undergraduate studies, whenever Freud was brought up, there was always a murmur of laughter, and a student would remark on "that old, crazy cocaine guy." To be honest with the reader, I was one of those students who contributed to those distastefully mistaken laughs. However, my opinion and attitude about Freud changed when, not surprisingly, I finally read some of his books. I strongly suggest reading his book "The Interpretation of Dreams" because, despite its enormous length, I came away with a new respect for his dedication to the development of the philosophy and science of behavior. I say this because it is just another example, and a personal one at that, that models the courage of behaving with intellectual humility and not being attached to being right all of the time. So before you judge Freud too harshly, make sure to at least read his work for yourself and get an understanding of where his ideas are coming from. For that matter, before judging anyone too harshly, try to understand them. This is a strong nudge to one of the themes of this book: perspective taking.

Chapter II

The New Philosophy

"If we can observe human behavior carefully from an objective point of view and come to understand it for what it is, we may be able to adopt a more sensible course of action." (1)

- B. F. Skinner

....

In the previous chapter, I introduced the mechanistic approach held by Hobbes and Petty, which was one of the most developmentally significant historical approaches, as it attempted to understand behavior as a function of the organism and argued for taking the spirits out of the body. I do not say this to take away from the achievements of others that I have discussed, or because I put them on a pedestal, but because it best sets up the ideas I will explicate in this chapter. That is, I discuss the philosophy that emphasizes the interaction of biology (nature) and the environment (nurture) in contributing to behavior. A mechanistic perspective brings with it a focus on both biology and the environment. There can be no more attributing things to a soul or an immaterial, willful spirit.

Yet, there is another approach, one that I have only named but not discussed in depth. I believe the most appropriate approach is one of functional analysis, and we cannot get into that without finally talking about radical behaviorism. I will use this lesson about radical behaviorism to motivate the key behaviors I am encouraging the reader to practice. As a reminder, they are *listening to and respecting others, perspective taking, honest self-expression, education, and courage.*

I also want to use this chapter to clarify some misguided views on Skinner and the work of behavior analysts. I have read many authors and scientists who would be screaming 'behaviorism is limited and incomplete!' yet simultaneously, and apparently unknowingly, supporting the same ideas that would appeal to a radical behaviorist. Situations like this, specifically referring to Sapolsky (whom I acknowledged in Chapter 1 as a critic of behaviorism), it is obvious that radical behaviorism, the work of B.F. Skinner, and other behaviorists or functional contextualists alike are still widely misunderstood.

Radical Behaviorism

To begin setting the record straight and prime the reader to best receive the message of this book, I will first formulate one sentence that encapsulates radical behaviorism. However, I hope the reader still works through this chapter, as there is much to radical behaviorism that the following sentence leaves out. It is the recognition of the inseparable entanglement of nature and nurture in regard to everything the organism is and does.

Radical behaviorism (hereafter RB) is not the science of human behavior but rather a *philosophy of that science* (2). With this philosophy, founder B.F. Skinner's main goal was to establish a framework in which the true causes of behavior are functional and contextual. Skinner sets out to explain in terms of organism-environment interaction why it is that organisms do what they do without appealing to ideas of the supernatural or free will. In this philosophy, everything that happens of the organism, including emotions, thoughts, dreams, neural and hormonal flux, etc., are considered behaviors and can be understood through functional analysis. Thus, rather than claiming that emotions, neurotransmitters, hormones, or even thoughts are the causes of behavior, RB interprets even things such as emotions, neurotransmitters, and hormone fluctuations, or even thoughts, *as behaviors* that themselves need to be explained and, more so, *can* be explained in terms of organism-environment interaction.

Behavior in the framework of RB, as I am trying to get across, is much broader in scope and more encompassing than behavior as it is commonly understood. Instead of behavior comprising only overt acts, such as walking, running, writing, talking, playing baseball, skateboarding, eating, etc., behavior in this sense is everything covert as well — all that the organism does internally in response to the environment. This idea of behavior includes everything that goes on inside the body, from heart rate, breathing, neurotransmitter flux, hormonal flux, to emotions, thoughts, and feelings. Radical behaviorists do not see any of these responses as causes of behavior but *as behaviors themselves.*

RB acknowledges that nothing happens in isolation, there are no inner causes to behavior, behavior is entirely context-specific, behavior is constrained by and allowed for by biology and a history of evolution, and responses can be explained without relying on free will. Skinner recognized the error in identifying biology as the sole cause of behavior, as well as the fallacy in overemphasizing the environment as the sole cause of behavior, as Locke did with the *tabula rasa*. Skinner and RB acknowledge that it is the interaction between biology and the environment, nature and nurture, that determines behavior.

Many people mistakenly believe that behaviorists do not think emotions are real, or that what goes on in the brain doesn't matter, but quite the contrary is true. RB, as mentioned above, acknowledges that these things happen, just not that they are the *cause* of anything. Emotions and feelings do not *cause* behaviors[4] but are behaviors themselves that can be explained by the organism–environment relationship—the two never being separated. RB simply recognizes emotions, thoughts, feelings, neural and hormonal flux, etc., as a response of the organism, which is constrained by biology, to the environment. RB is a simple philosophy that recognizes the complete intertwinement of nature *and* nurture. It holds that emotions and brain activity are *responses of the organism* and are merely the first responses in a chain of organism-wide reactions, all of which are context-specific and constrained by biology.

---

[4] This is a mentalistic approach that exhibits an attachment to the idea of free will and humans acting independent of the world.

RB does not ignore what exists under the skin, as Skinner puts it, or attribute emotions (or other private events, such as consciousness, memories, thoughts, or beliefs) to the nonphysical "black box" so commonly propagated by mentalists. This black box refers to the mind and its unapproachable nature, which are presented as subjects that cannot be studied scientifically. Rather than this blindly faithful idea, RB attempts to explain emotions (and all other private events) *not as causes of behavior but as behavior itself*. In other words, the *origins* of all behaviors can be explained, not by some internal volition, but by the contingencies of survival as described by Darwin in his theory of natural selection, the contingencies of reinforcement as described by Pavlov, and, as I will show in Chapter Three, Skinner (3). This is the basic overview of radical behaviorism. With this approach, we can see the acknowledgment of humans, and all organisms, as entities forever entangled with the environment, never becoming separate from the natural world, never isolated.

Biology

One of the major critiques of RB is that "it ignores biology." However, this is simply not true; it just does not see biology as the sole *cause* of behavior. RB recognizes biology but only as half of the equation, with the other half being the environment (the two parts in nature and nurture). As I have said earlier, RB holds that all biological responses that occur inside the body are related to the organism's environment and have context-based functions, even including gene activation. It is worth reiterating that brain activity, the nervous system, and even gene activation *are not the causes* of behavior but biological responses of the organism to the environment in a chain of reactions. As I will demonstrate, everything biological, from heart rates to dopamine rushes, is context-specific.

Now, what do I mean by saying that biological responses are context-specific? I mean precisely that reflexes, brain activation, neurotransmitters and hormone flux, and gene activation, for example, are responses of the organism contingent on the environment, and that they do not occur in solitude. The biology of the organism is not isolated from the rest of the world or "doing its own thing." An organism's biology and the environment are intimately married and have made unbreakable vows.

Let's look at hormones, as so many people like to attribute our behavior to them. Many people say that it is because of testosterone that males are more aggressive, suggesting that testosterone causes the aggression. This is a simplistic view of human behavior, and it is time to show how wrong this is.[5] For example, what about someone who has been chemically castrated? Can they no longer be aggressive now because of their lack of testosterone? If someone reasons that testosterone is the cause of aggression, then it would stand to reason that someone with either inhibited testosterone production or blocked testosterone receptors would not be aggressive. Their reasoning is that without testosterone to cause the aggression, there cannot be aggression. However, this is not what we see. A deeper empirical analysis of

---

[5] I am pulling this testosterone example from Sapolsky's book *Behave* to finally show specifically how Sapolsky argues like a radical behaviorist, albeit unwillingly.

castration and aggression shows that the more experience a male had being aggressive prior to castration, the more aggression continues afterward. The less his being aggressive in the future requires testosterone, the more it's a product of environmental contingencies! Aggression is less about testosterone and more about the contexts in which aggressive behavior is reinforced. As one meta-analysis concluded, "hostile rapists and those who commit sex crimes motivated by power or anger are not amenable to treatment with...[the antiandrogenic drugs]." This acknowledges that castration does not "cure" someone of their aggressive behavior. Thus, it is not biology that is the problem but the history of aggression being reinforced. Furthermore, it has been shown that high basal levels of testosterone have little to do with aggression. This is why increases in testosterone due to puberty and sex do not increase aggression (4). Thus, if we look for the cause of aggression inside the organism, isolating its biology from the outside world, we will not find it; we must look toward the environment as well. As RB suggests, we must recognize that all of the organisms' responses happen in context.

This castration example is useful for showing that testosterone fluctuation, a biological response of the organism, is not the cause of behavior. However, this example contributes little to explaining how testosterone secretion is context-specific. To illuminate the contextual function of testosterone fluctuation, allow me to discuss some of the many ways testosterone is related to different behaviors. For starters, what are the reasons, other than aggression, that testosterone levels increase? First, when we "win" at something or accomplish a goal, we see an increase in testosterone secretion.

Success in everything from athletics to chess to the stock market boosts testosterone levels; accomplishing an aim increases testosterone. (5) In addition, anxiety increases testosterone – if you are in a threatening environment, you become more reactively aggressive. Additionally, taking risks increases testosterone – "Hey, let's gamble." (6) Whether it is attributable to accomplishing a goal, feeling anxiety, or taking risks, the release of testosterone is all about the context. Testosterone flux does not occur in isolation or at random but instead as a response to some change in the environment. Context, context, context. This all supports the RB idea that hormone flux is not the cause of behavior – rather, it *is* a behavior (a response of the organism) that is contingent upon the environment.

Now, what about neurotransmitters? This is another biological response of the organism that people too often credit as the cause of behavior. RB argues that neurotransmitter flux, just like hormonal flux, should be viewed as a response of the organism to its environmental context. Neural flux is not the cause but *the effect* – the first response in a chain of responses. Just as testosterone is not the cause of behavior but a response to some environmental occurrence, so is neural flux. To be perfectly clear, dopamine, for example, does not cause behavior; dopamine flux itself is a response of the organism (a behavior) that can be understood by analyzing the relationship between the biology of the organism and its environment. RB does not ignore neurotransmitters or claim that they are not important in behavior. Rather, it simply sees them like any other response of the organism, with its origins explained by contingencies of survival (natural   selection)   and   contingencies   of reinforcement (conditioning).

What about genes? Well, genes themselves are not behavior, but their activation is. The reason for this is that gene activation is also highly context-specific and always takes place in relation to the environment. Genes do not determine behavior; rather, they allow and constrain behaviors. Genes originated   because   of   natural   selection (contingencies of survival), and their moment-to-moment changes in expression are caused by their environmental   context   (contingencies   of reinforcement). [6] RB does not believe that genes determine everything, as they are only half of the equation. The other half, again, is the environment! I repeat this point so it is clear: behavior is never just biology and never just the environment but a constant interaction between the two that is never isolated.

The main point of this section is to get the reader to understand that what goes on under the skin — i.e., biology, with its neurotransmitters, hormones, and genes — is not the cause of behavior. Rather, the biological responses of the organism are behaviors that can be explained in the same way that all other behaviors can be explained — by looking at the relationship between the organism (and all its biology) and the environment. As Skinner says in his book *Science and Human Behavior*, "we operate in one world" where

---

[6] I say "because" to remain consistent with RB that nothing is solely "because" of just one thing but rather a cumulative process.

behavior is the "coherent, continuous activity of an integral organism." (7)

Going Forward

I did my best to keep this chapter short and to the point, without getting too carried away any one nuance of this philosophy. If the reader really wants to take a deep dive into the work of Skinner, I highly recommend reading his book *About Behaviorism,* as it does go into depths too detailed for this chapter. But forewarning, Skinner was never the best at easily portraying his ideas to the public (which is why behaviorism is still misunderstood), so it might be a challenging read. Hopefully, though, for those who have been misguided about behaviorism in the past, I hope this has been clarifying.

To summarize, this chapter has been about radical behaviorism, or the philosophy of the science of behavior developed by B. F. Skinner. I have been trying to drill home the key point of nature and nurture being in a harmonious relationship throughout the whole process of behavior, never separating and never leaving room for free will. Still, I have yet to talk about the science of behavior that Skinner described. That is for the next chapter, where I will give a basic account of Skinner's operant conditioning, the foundation for a functional analysis of behavior. I have been talking a lot about behavior being context-specific and have mentioned 'contingencies of reinforcement', but I have yet to give a detailed account for either. It is time to do so.

Coda

A few weeks after I finished writing the second draft of this book, I was able to schedule a meeting with Dr. Steven Hayes to talk about the publishing process for the book. As someone who started his own publishing company on top of publishing close to 50 books, he was able to give me some great tips and guide me in the publishing process, and for that, I am grateful. This being so, I must pay my respects and give a quick review of Dr. Hayes' background since, after all, it is his work that I decided to study in my undergraduate years at the University of Nevada, Reno.

The first thing you should know about him is that he is one of the most cited academics in any field of study... ever! He developed a new theory of human language called relational frame theory, which he extended into one of the most successful clinical therapies to date: acceptance and commitment therapy, or ACT (said as one word). But he did not stop there; with over 600 published articles, he continued to co-develop another clinical approach, what I predict to be an even more successful, called process-based therapy. Only time will tell whether this is so.

I bring up my talk with Dr. Hayes at the end of this chapter, specifically, because after we discussed aspects of the publishing process, we started talking about the content of this book, which helped me tremendously. Our conversation focused on radical behaviorism and something called functional contextualism. At first, I was worried that the latter might be a completely different approach than radical behaviorism, and not only would I have to reframe my own personal theoretical orientation—I would have to rewrite this book! But to my delight and relief, functional contextualism is basically a clarification of radical behaviorism, for as I have said, Skinner's work was not well understood and was highly misinterpreted.

To recap the basics of radical behaviorism, everything an organism does *is* behavior, and an organism always behaves in the context of an environment. Functional contextualism, however, really focuses on the point that, when analyzing behavior, we should be more concerned with the *function* of behavior rather than the form of it (topography), and to know the function of the behavior, we must look at the context in which the behavior happens. Thus, functional contextualism is the kangaroo child of radical behaviorism, housed in its mother's pouch, and has a better, clearer name.

While editing this chapter, I restructured some of the vocabulary to reflect the functionally contextual view that is housed inside radical behaviorism. However, for the most part, the ideas of this chapter held strong, and I did not have to change any of the main points of this chapter or of the book at large. Thus, the idea still stands that organisms behave, not because of free will but because of the natural processes of nature that allow the organism to function as it does in its specific context — nature and nurture, the organism and the environment, never separate and always working in cahoots.

Chapter III

Selecting Behavior

"It's not our fault that our minds work this way." (1)
- Dr. Steven Hayes

....

In the first chapter, I showed how historical figures have struggled to understand and explain behavior. We discussed the findings of Pavlov (classical/respondent conditioning), how animals learn to respond to neutral stimuli when paired with an unconditioned stimulus, and how animals learn through association in space and time (something that happens "unconsciously"). As a quick refresher, respondent conditioning occurs when two stimuli are paired in space and time so that the function of one is transferred to the other (the stimulus function is transferred to the neutral stimulus). Think back to Pavlov's dogs and the bell; the bell had no function until it was consistently paired with food, and eventually, the bell took on the same stimulus function as the food, and the dogs salivated just at the ringing of the bell. The previously neutral stimulus, the bell, took on the same function as the food, eliciting salivation from the dogs. This was a truly groundbreaking, if accidental, discovery. Pavlov showed how behaviors (or reflexes, at least) are selected by the environment on an individual level, taking the idea of free will out of the equation.

I introduce this chapter in this way because I cannot state enough how important the ability is of an individual organism to learn and have its behavior shaped during its lifetime – this is the nurture aspect of behavior. At this point in history with Pavlov, we have just gotten the biggest piece of evidence that shows organisms are not freely behaving with inner volition. That there is a method to the madness, an explanation of why organisms behave as they do, other than some internal "want" or "will." Pavlov's dogs did not "choose" to start salivating to the bell; rather, they did so because of their genetic endowment, which allows for classical conditioning (or contingencies of survival, as described by Darwin).

Still, as groundbreaking as the findings of Pavlov are, there is more to be discovered about behavior and how organisms learn from the environment. Not all behavior can be conceptualized as a reflex, and not all conditioning is a transfer of stimulus control. There is more to the equation.

This is a good introduction to Burrhus Frederic Skinner, who, in 1938, published his book *The Behavior of Organisms* detailing his newfound approach of how organisms learn from the environment. He called his new approach "operant conditioning," which details how organisms learn from consequences and other environmental variables. Along with this new kind of conditioning came a new category of behavior, broadening our vocabulary and articulation of nature. Justly named "operant behavior," this distinction between behavior and reflex is not a mere stimulus–response relationship but is instead more context-dependent.

To distinguish between a reflex and operant behavior, we could say that an operant behavior is "emitted" by the organism, while a reflex is "elicited." Stimuli do not elicit an operant behavior automatically like a reflex; instead, operant behavior is simply made more probable following reinforcement (a concept that I will focus on in this chapter).

Rather than just looking at what happens at the same time in space (as Pavlov did), Skinner's operant conditioning looks at what happens *before and after* a response as well, or the *antecedents and consequences* preceding and following a response. This revolutionary analysis of organism–environment interaction has not only had an extraordinary impact on the field of psychology but has also been groundbreaking for helping those with learning disabilities (such as autism). The application of Skinner's operant conditioning, known as applied behavior analysis (ABA), is the only evidence-based approach that has stood the test of time as a way of bettering the lives of those with autism. As a registered behavior technician in the great state of Nevada, I have personally used ABA (the application of Skinner's operant conditioning) on a daily basis when teaching kids with autism to do basically anything and everything that I and the reader (who I assume does not have a learning disability) take for granted. For example, I have used ABA to teach kids how to brush their hair, fold their clothes, put away the dishes, fill a bag of chips to a certain level so they can close the bag without crushing all of the chips, talk about their favorite places, have conversations, turn off an alarm, politely interrupt others, respond appropriately to others' emotions, use proper tones of voice, compromise, share, ask for help, respect personal space, wash their hands, and an innumerable list of other skills and tasks of daily living that have life-changing benefits for clients.

Now, in this chapter, I will provide the long-awaited expansion on operant conditioning, what it is, and why it is so important for this book's theme of cooperation. However, before getting into the thick of it, I must clearly state the most important thing to know about operant conditioning: it *describes the process of behavior selection on an individual level, supplementing natural selection* (2). An operant condition is not the *cause* of behavior but simply describes a relationship between the environment and the organism. Without being technical, operant conditioning is part of the second half of the equation to behavior—the nurture aspect. Remember when I said there is a method to the madness? Well, this is one of the best descriptions of that method to date.

The A-B-Cs of Operant Conditioning

There is no better place to start talking about operant conditioning than with the three-term contingency. This is the bedrock of operant conditioning. Remember a few paragraphs ago when I said that Skinner's operant conditioning looks at what happens *before and after* a response or the *antecedents and consequences* preceding and following a response? Well, the three-term contingency describes exactly this. In operant conditioning, we look at the environment before a response, or the antecedent context; we look at the response itself, or the behavior; and then we look at the environment after the response, or the consequence. Spelled out, that is A (antecedent), B (behavior or response), and C (consequence), properly known as the ABCs of operant conditioning.

An **antecedent** is defined as *an event or stimulus that precedes some other event or stimulus and often emits, signals, or sets the occasion for a particular behavior or response* (3). Without all the jargon, an antecedent is the context in which a behavior happens. To better describe this, it will help to use an example that the reader is probably familiar with. Imagine being at breakfast, and a family member or friend requests of you to pass them the butter, saying, "Please pass me the butter." Assuming you do so, the antecedent in this situation is being at breakfast with that family member or friend and being asked to pass the butter.[7] In this situation, you pass the butter not because of a decision to exercise free will but because in that context, the behavior of passing the butter has been made more probable through the process of reinforcement (a concept I will discuss shortly). Most likely, you would not have passed the butter to your family member or friend at that exact time if they did not request you to do so. You might, however, still pass the butter without them

---

[7] The main antecedent is intermixed with a plethora of other unidentified variables that may or may not be influencing your decision to pass the butter. I will get into other contextual variables later in this chapter that can influence behavior, namely motivation.

directly requesting it of you, but even in that case, there would still be other variables in the antecedent context we could look to for an explanation. For example, maybe that family member or friend always asks you to pass the butter after they finish eating their first appetizer. So, this time, before they even finish chewing their last bite of that appetizer, you pass the butter to them, in a sense, anticipating them asking. Thus, everything, including passing butter to a family member at breakfast, is context-specific, and we describe that context with the word "antecedent."

A **behavior** is defined as *an organism's activities in response to external or internal stimuli, including objectively observable activities, introspectively observable activities, and nonconscious processes* (4). Broken down, behavior is what I have been referring to as "the response of the organism" to some environmental context. It is everything that the organism does. Remember, organisms never respond in isolation; any and all responses of the organism happen in relationship to the environment. The behavior analyst's approach to behavior is much different than that of an ordinary person, which is why this definition of behavior may be confusing at first. Under this definition, responses such as emotions and thoughts are included as behaviors and can be examined by environment–organism contingencies. Neurotransmitter flux, hormonal flux, brain activation, emotions, thoughts, feelings, and dreams are all responses of the organism and are thus understood to be behaviors.

A **consequence** is *a stimulus change after behavior* (5). Take out the fancy slang, and this refers to whatever happens after a response, or how the environment changes after the behavior occurs.

Back to our butter-passing example, after passing the butter, what happens next? Does the family member say, "Thank you," utter a snarky comment or something passive aggressive, or do nothing at all? Whichever it is, these are all examples of changes in the environment that could happen after passing the butter, all of which will affect future behavior. Notice that, whatever it is, consequences are inevitable; as long as time keeps ticking away, there will be consequences for every action.

Now, before going deeper into the woods of operant conditioning and how consequences affect the future probability of behaving, I want to note the colloquial misuse of "consequence" and clear up the issue. Too often, people use "consequence" as synonymous with "punishment," as if to face the consequences of one's actions means to face reprimands or punishment for doing something "bad." We see this when parents say that their child needs to "face the consequences of their actions" when their child does something "wrong" (like stealing from a store), as if consequences are only things that are "bad" or punishable. People will say that those who break the law need to "face the consequence of their actions," again, as if consequences only mean something that happens to someone after they do something "bad." This mistake troubles me.

I will try to clear this mess up here. A consequence is not always something "bad" or punishable, despite the epidemic of colloquial misuse. Yes, consequences can be punishable or bad, but consequences are not always punishing or bad. [8] Consequences, most of the time, can be *reinforcing,* which are usually described as something that feels good. Consequences are not just for when someone does something bad but are for when someone does something good, too. If a parent sees that their child has taken out the trash, there is a consequence of that action (maybe a hug, a thank you, an allowance, or nothing at all). If a person does something to help the public, there are consequences of that as well (such as tax write-offs or distinguished honors). In ABA, we call this "catching someone doing good." This is the side of consequences that goes unrecognized in this colloquial misuse.

Consequences are not "good" or "bad," and there is no subjectivity when it comes to consequences. Rather, consequences, with no emotional bias to one's morals or ethics, simply describe what happens after someone does something (literally anything!). If someone does something against the law, those consequences will likeliest be jail, prison time, or a fine. However, if someone does something that is approved of by others, those consequences will likely be praise, attention, and possibly even money.

Now, these are the three terms of the three-term contingency, but the reader might still be left wondering what a contingency is. A **contingency** is simply *a description of the relationship between environmental events and an organisms' actions.* Specifically, a contingency in this context is a relationship between the three parts just described.

---

[8] RB adherents never use the subjective terms "good" or "bad" when describing a consequence. I only do so here because they are terms we can easily understand.

Again, they are the environment before a response, the response of an organism, and the environment after the response. In terms of behavior analysis, a contingency is the relationship between an antecedent, behavior, and consequence. The reader should note, however, that contingencies are not causes of behavior. Rather, a contingency is *a description of a process*, where that process is the selection of behavior at the level of an individual. The two big processes, reinforcement and punishment, will be the focus of the next section.

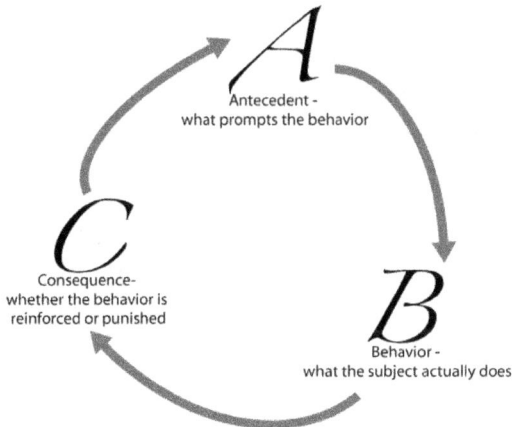

A

Antecedent -
what prompts the behavior

C

Consequence-
whether the behavior is
reinforced or punished

B

Behavior -
what the subject actually does

Figure 1. Notice that the consequence of one action becomes the antecedent for the next response. Because the three-term contingency is an analysis over time, what comes after a behavior, the consequence, will now be the new current context, or antecedent, for the next behavior, which produces another consequence, and so on.

Contingencies of Reinforcement and Punishment

It is now time to talk about the bread and butter of operant conditioning: reinforcement and punishment. I have just gone over how consequences are what happen after a response—a family member says "thank you" after you pass them the butter—but have yet to discuss the different kinds of consequences and their effects on the behavior they follow. As I said when talking about the colloquial misuse of the word "consequence," a consequence can be either reinforcing or punishing. How the family member responds after you pass them the butter will influence your likelihood of passing them the butter in the future. What they say can increase, maintain, or decrease the future probability of passing the butter. If they say, "Thank you," one can imagine that this will increase your likelihood of passing them butter in the future. However, if they say something snarky or passive-aggressive, one can predict that your likelihood of passing them the butter will decrease (yet we will not know this until we observe the future behavior). Each consequence carries with it a different future.

Reinforcement is *the process in which the frequency or probability of a response is increased by a dependent relationship, or contingency, with a stimulus or circumstance* (7). Meanwhile, a **reinforcer** is *a stimulus or circumstance that produces reinforcement when it occurs in a dependent relationship, or contingency, with a response* (6). Reinforcement is the process of strengthening behavior, and a reinforcer is what helps create that change. A reinforcer is the thing/event, whereas reinforcement is the process of increasing the future probability of that response in similar contexts.

But what if the butter-passing situation was different? What if, instead of saying, "Thank you," the family member said something snarky? Presume you don't like the snarky comment (you find it aversive), and the frequency of passing butter *decreases* in the future; this scenario can be described as punishing. **Punishment** is *the process in which the relationship, or contingency, between a response and some stimulus or circumstance results in the response becoming* <u>less probable</u> (8). In other words, punishment is the opposite of reinforcement. Instead of a consequence that increases future probability, as a reinforcer does, a punishing consequence decreases the probability of future behavior in such a context.

To summarize, a consequence is either said to be reinforcing or punishing. This classification is not based on any emotions or morals but rather just by what happens to the future probability of the behavior it follows. This is as objective as it comes. A consequence that increases the future probability of the response it follows is a reinforcer, while something that decreases the future probability of the response a consequence follows is a punisher. Reinforcement and punishment are processes of operant behavior selection.

Before moving on to the other two dimensions of consequences (positive and negative), I want to hammer in this last point. Something is either reinforcing or punishing based on how it affects the behavior it follows, *not* on how someone *believes* it will affect the behavior. For example, for those who go to prison and reoffend once released, and continually reoffend and get shipped off to prison, a prison sentence cannot be called punishment. The frequency of that criminal behavior did not decrease! Just because someone thinks that going to prison is "bad" does not mean that any punishment is happening. This is why radical behaviorists do not analyze consequences with subjective terms, such as "good" or "bad." Instead, behavior analysts look to quantitative measurements to see if there has been any statistically significant change in behavior following the consequences. Still, it is only after observing future behavior that one can identify reinforcement or punishment.

Positive and Negative

Not only are these the last two dimensions in labeling a consequence, but these next two terms vie for the crown of being most misunderstood: positive and negative. A *positive* consequence is not some subjective "good," nor is a *negative* consequence some subjective "bad." "Positive" and "negative" have nothing to do with any one person's feelings, morals, ethics, or opinions about right or wrong, good or bad, happiness or sadness. While taking my AP psychology class in high school, I made this mistake, which is yet another example of me trying to model for the reader the behavior of intellectual humility. I can admit that I have been wrong in the past, and that I will continue to be wrong in the future, but I continue to value education and am constantly motivated to right my intellectual wrongs.

The other previously mentioned dimensions of consequences, reinforcement and punishment, describe changes in future behavior, whereas the dimensions of positive and negative describe how a behavior changes the stimuli in its environment. Specifically, it refers to whether a behavior introduces the organism to a stimulus or a behavior removes them from a stimulus. Now, without the technical behavior analytic gibberish, I mean that a positive consequence describes when the organism receives or gains access to something, and a negative consequence describes when the organism loses or escapes from something. Instead of thinking of positive and negative in emotionally subjective terms, such as good and bad, think about them more as addition and subtraction, respectively.

Using the butter example again, being told "thank you" is a positive consequence of passing the butter. Not because being told "thank you" feels good or makes you happy but because it is a newly added stimulus in your environment. Furthermore, handing off the butter is described as a negative consequence. Not because you feel bad about giving up the butter but because a stimulus is being removed once you let go. Thus, a behavior can have both positive and negative consequences. Passing the butter both removes the butter from your possession and grants access to the receipt of gratitude from whomever you passed the butter to. Think about how, whenever you buy something, there is the negative consequence of giving up your money as well as the positive consequence of receiving the product you have just purchased. In neither case do "positive" or "negative" refer to feelings or emotions about what is happening but to the objective and measurable changes in the environment.

Here are some more examples to help nail down the concept. Imagine that a child takes out the trash (response) when his mother requests him to do so (antecedent). Consequently, the mother gives the child his allowance. This situation, receiving money, can be described as the *addition* of a stimulus following a response, and thus a positive consequence. Now, to determine whether the consequence is reinforcing or punishing, we must look at the future frequency of taking out the trash when asked. If taking out the trash increases or maintains its frequency in the future, this would be described as *positive reinforcement*, which is what I would predict.

Now imagine that a child does *not* take out the trash upon the mothers' request. Maybe they are scrolling aimlessly through social media. As a consequence, the mom takes away the child's phone and tells them that they will get it back once they take out the trash (establishing a rule). The child's loss of access to their phone is a *negative* consequence. The child then proceeds to take out the trash and is granted back their phone afterwards. The child gaining back access to their phone is a *positive* consequence.

	Punishment (decreasing behavior)	Reinforcement (increasing behavior)
Positive (adding)	adding something to decrease behavior	adding something to increase behavior
Negative (subtracting)	subtracting something to decrease behavior	subtracting something to increase behavior

Schedules of Reinforcement

There is one more thing we must cover to get a better idea of how consequences affect behavior. Now, since we have gone over the three-term contingency (the ABCs of operant conditioning) and positive and negative reinforcement and punishment (our bread and butter), it is time to talk about schedules of reinforcement, or the different ways a consequence can be delivered contingent upon behavior. This is less of what the consequence is and more of a description of when the consequence happens.

Properly defined, **schedules of reinforcement** are *the procedures for arranging reinforcers in time and in relation to responses* (13). In other words, this is how consequences are delivered after a behavior. As simple of a factor as this may seem, how reinforcement is delivered has unavoidable, and important, impacts on behavior. For instance, is a reinforcer given after every correct response **(continuous reinforcement)**? After a certain number of responses **(fixed ratio)**? After an average number of responses **(variable ratio)**? After a certain amount of time **(fixed interval)**? After an average amount of time **(variable interval)**? Notice how each schedule is an assortment of fixed or variable and interval or ratio. Each different kind of schedule results in a specific pattern of responses that is unique to the kind of schedule.

The most important aspect of these different schedules is the impact they have on the frequency of behavior. Based on which schedule is in effect, behavior will vary in relation to that schedule. Starting with the interval schedules, fixed interval schedules (reinforcement after a set interval of time) are characterized by a moderate response rate, with significant pauses after reinforcement. For this schedule, think of a child who receives their allowance once a week if their room is cleaned up. We can expect that they will wait until the last minute of Friday night to clean their room, just in the nick of time to get paid. On the other hand, variable interval schedules (reinforcement after an average interval of time) are characterized by a moderate yet steady response rate. For this schedule, think of a child who earns their allowance at random. Sometimes they receive it at the end of the week, and sometimes it takes their parents a week and a half to pay up, but sometimes it only takes half a week to get paid. There is an average of receiving an allowance once per week, but it can vary. For the ratio schedules, fixed ratio schedules (reinforcement after a set number of responses) are characterized by a high response rate with pauses after reinforcement. For example, with every three chores a child completes, they receive their allowance right then and there after completing the third chore — no waiting until the end of the week. Finally, variable ratio schedules (reinforcement after an average number of responses) are characterized by the high and steady response rates commonly seen in gambling behavior. This would be if the child receives their allowance on an average of every three chores they complete; sometimes they receive it after one or two chores, but then again, sometimes they receive it after four or five chores (14).

For those readers who are well versed in behavior analysis, this should be a simple review, but for those who have never heard of the concept of schedules of reinforcement, this might be utterly overwhelming. In the case of the latter, my goal is simply to explain these ideas to underline that

behavior is largely dependent upon environmental
factors outside the control of the individual.

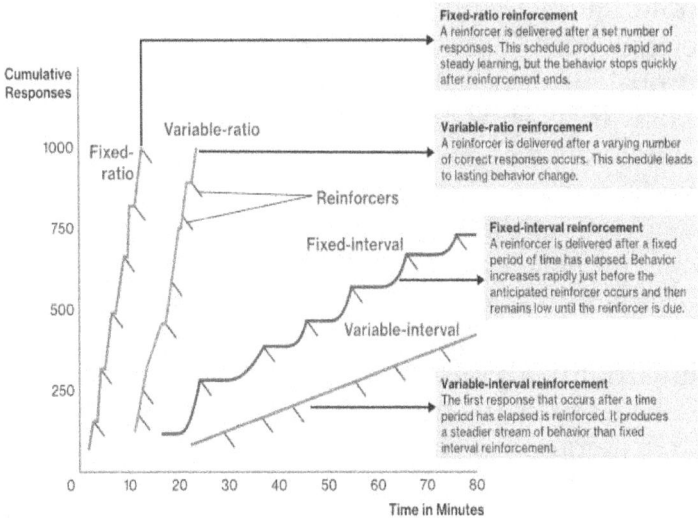

Fixed-ratio reinforcement
A reinforcer is delivered after a set number of
responses. This schedule produces rapid and
steady learning, but the behavior stops quickly
after reinforcement ends.

Variable-ratio reinforcement
A reinforcer is delivered after a varying number
of correct responses occurs. This schedule leads
to lasting behavior change.

Fixed-interval reinforcement
A reinforcer is delivered after a fixed
period of time has elapsed. Behavior
increases rapidly just before the
anticipated reinforcer occurs and then
remains low until the reinforcer is due.

Variable-interval reinforcement
The first response that occurs after a time
period has elapsed is reinforced. It produces
a steadier stream of behavior than fixed
interval reinforcement.

Motivation

Before wrapping up this chapter, we still need to
cover one more major component of operant
conditioning that describes how operant behavior
is selected. I have done much to expand on
consequences, but now I want to expand on how
the environmental context at the time of behavior
affects behavior. It is time to talk about motivation.
This is yet another concept that is widely misused
outside the behavior analytic community. [9]
Contrary to its colloquial use, motivation is not a
measure of how "lazy" or "excited" someone is or
isn't. Nor is motivation about "willpower" or a

---

[9] By now, you might have caught on to the theme that many
terms in behavior analysis are widely misunderstood and
misused. This is a situation I aim to rectify with this book.

reflection of one's "moral character." Instead of all this mentalist mumbo jumbo about some "internal" factor that drives behavior, motivation is about how a setting, or context, influences the effectiveness of consequences, and thus the probability of behaviors. In plain English, motivation is not about the organism but rather about the circumstances in which the organism finds itself.

Motivation is defined as *the variables that collectively alter the effectiveness of reinforcers* (9). Basically, this is how the totality of the situation preceding a behavior affects how valuable (or important) a consequence is. It reflects what is referred to as the need to behave in such a way as to experience a desired consequence. Thus, in relation to the ABCs, motivation can rightly be thought of as a factor that comes before the antecedent, or a condition that overlays the rest of the environmental context (written as M: [A-B-C]). Analyzing the motivating factors helps explain the context-specificity of behavior, why behavior might vary in what may seem to be the same exact antecedent conditions, and even our most intense behavior of desperation.

Motivation is crucial for understanding when a stimulus or consequence serves as a reinforcer. Let's take the basic example of the eating behavior of rats in a lab. Food will function as a reinforcer only if the rats are "hungry" or *deprived* of food. What this looks like is an increase in behavior that gives them access to food (this might be pressing a button). On the other hand, if the rats are "full" or *satiated*, then food will not be as valuable and will not function as a reinforcer at that time. This manifests itself as a decrease in the behavior that gives them access to food (now, they press the button less or not at all). In this example, the rat being deprived of, or denied access to, food is an **establishing operation,** or *an event change that increases the effectiveness of reinforcement supporting operant behavior* (10). Meanwhile, the scenario in which the rat is satiated is an **abolishing operation,** or *an event that decreases the effectiveness of the consequent stimuli* (11). Being hungry did not cause the button-pushing behavior, nor did being full cause the behavior to stop. Rather, each respective factor made the consequence of gaining access to food more or less valuable, and thus more or less probable to occur at that point in time.

Now, this next exercise may seem a little bizarre, but it will clearly show what motivation is for a behavior analyst. Ask yourself, under what conditions might you cut off your own arm? No seriously. Would you do it just for the fun of it? Probably not. Maybe because your friends ask you to? Again, probably not. Maybe because a stranger offers you 10 billion dollars? Still, probably not (but then again, that 10 billion dollars might be the right motivating factor for some people). You might be thinking that there is no circumstance in which you would have the "will" to dismember your own limb, but think again.

Imagine you were stuck, trapped, abandoned, pinned against a boulder in a dark crevasse in the remote desert, and the only hope of freeing yourself and getting to safety is brutally sawing off your own arm. Would you do it? This is no longer a hypothetical; in fact, this is the exact situation in which a mountain climber by the name of Aron Ralston found himself in (12). After spending 127 hours hopelessly waiting for a rescue team to arrive that never showed, he did what most people would quiver in fear and disgust at (even if offered 10 billion dollars). He amputated his own arm and freed himself from the boulder.[10]

So, what is motivation? In the context of Aron, motivation is the accumulation of each second without communication with a rescue team, every minute that goes by without budging from the boulder, and every day that goes by without food or water. Motivation, more specifically, an establishing operation, is every factor that influences Aron's "will to survive" — or in more behavioral terms, the functional value of cutting off his own arm. The longer Aron spent trapped, the more valuable freedom became. The longer he went without food, the more valuable food became. The longer without water, the more valuable water became. The closer he was to death, survival became all the more valuable, and any behaviors that had a survival function became all the more likely. Motivation is the compounding set of factors that influenced his choice to cut off his own arm instead of dying alone. If you have ever questioned or wondered about the extremes people, or even you, would go to survive, look at this motivation. Given the proper circumstances, humans will do unimaginable things to survive. Humans will run six miles, barefoot, through the snow, if the circumstances are put in place.[11] You do not know

---

[10] Still, he was not completely free, as he had yet to climb out of the crevasse he had fallen into while limited to only one arm.

[11] This is a reference to the movie *Wind River* in which a Native American girl escapes her rapist but dies from the cold after running six miles, barefoot, through the snow of Montana. This is a truly incredible yet disturbing testament to the human species, for better and for worse.

what you are capable of until you are put in the position to do it.

Going Forward

Take this introduction to operant conditioning with a grain of salt, as it does not fully encapsulate all the nuances in operant conditioning and behavior analysis. There are many more important concepts (such as stimulus and response, discrimination and generalization, rule-governed behavior, and shaping, to name a few) that I did not cover. Yet, granted this chapter's brevity, it still provides a preliminary understanding of how and why animals behave as they do given their environment and history in that environment. [12] Now, going forward, every time I mention that individual uniqueness is partly and largely because of one's environmental history (constrained by genetics, of course), I specifically mean because of the process that operant (and respondent) conditioning describes.

---

[12] Remember, this chapter was solely on operant conditioning; animals also behave according to respondent (Pavlovian) conditioning, as well as genetic endowment. Skinner and behavior analysts alike do not ignore these other explanatory factors of behavior but rather incorporate them into one large umbrella of radical behaviorism.

Chapter IV

Free will (or the lack thereof)

"A man likes to believe that he is the master of his soul."
(1)

- Carl G. Jung

....

I can predict that this chapter will be the most controversial part of this book, not because it is incorrect, but because it is an idea to which many of us are deeply attached. This chapter will be provocative to that standard. Thus, I will reassure the reader that this chapter is not an attack on any belief, nor is it to be taken as anti-religious rhetoric. Rather, this is simply a breakdown of the implications of radical behaviorism. I make this the last chapter of Part One for an important reason: it is through this implication of RB that I will show the value of *listening to and respecting others, appreciation for new perspectives, honest self-expression, education, and courage.*

In this chapter, I will defend the claim that people do not behave as they do because of a "want," "will," "purpose," or 'intention'; there are no "mental causes" of behavior; the body is not moved by any "indwelling spirits,"; and choice is not the exercise of free will. To be clear, when I say that free will does not exist, I simply mean that people's behaviors are selected by contingencies of reinforcement instead of inner self-causes (similar to Darwin's theory of natural selection). Assuming you have read everything up to this point in the book, and I have made myself clear, the reader should have a pretty good idea of why I am going to defend these claims. But before going any further, I want to put forth a definition so we can all be on the same page, since I have not done so already. The American Psychological Association (APA) defines **free will** as *the power or capacity of a human being for self-direction* (2). More simply, free will can be thought of as free choice — roughly, the ability to "do what you want" and "be in control." In behavioral terms, this notion of free will is thought to refer to a person's ability to make choices independent of contingencies and schedules of reinforcement. This means that you can give a person a set of options and they will be able to make a choice, regardless of their environmental history. As you might imagine, I and RB adherents alike disagree with this notion and have no shortage of ammunition to defend this position. That being the case, this chapter has two purposes: providing a behavior-analytic description of why people make the choices they do without attributing anything to free will and clarifying the implications of what a lack of free will entails.

Choice

Choice is often seen as an exertion of free will and the ability to act morally, ethically, or wisely — something of a voluntary decision. Mentalists will say that a person chooses to do something because they "want to," "feel compelled to," or even "intend to," as if there is some inner mini-homunculus trapped in the basement of their brain or an immaterial spirit calling the shots. If this were to be the case, it implies some seriously degrading things about people who suffer from depression or anxiety. Assuming there is free will also assumes that someone lacks the "will" to pull themselves out of their depressed state. Needless to say, this is a pretty crummy view of depression and one I do not support. To a behaviorist, however, this is not the case — something the reader could have probably guessed by now. To repeat myself, behavior analysts see decision-making as being controlled by contingencies of reinforcement, specifically schedules of reinforcement, which are completely intertwined with and dependent on the environment. This is the exact point I have been hammering home in the previous two chapters. But what do I mean when I say that choice is determined by schedules of reinforcement? To start to explain this, let's look at what choice is to a behavior analyst since it is probably much different than how most people think of it (how fitting of a theme — another concept that is understood differently by behavior analysts and the general public).

Choice is *the distribution of operant behavior among alternative sources of reinforcement.* (3)[13] This is a fancy way of characterizing the probability of choosing each option, or how likely one is to respond in a certain way. This can be referred to more succinctly as the availability of multiple different behaviors at the same time.

With this availability of multiple options at the same time comes variability and uncertainty — indeed, the uncertainty is what makes it so interesting to study. For this reason, I like to compare choice behavior in psychology to quantum mechanics in physics in that they both work in the realm of probability, not certainty. There is only likelihood, possibility, and odds — increases and decreases in future probability based on past experience with those options and current conditions.[14]

We can describe how likely one is to choose each available option but not which option *will* be chosen. This means that if someone is predicted to choose option A 80% of the time, over 100 trials,

---

[13] Please note that this means choice is specific to operant behavior. Reflexes are simple stimulus-response relationships. Therefore, there is only one possible response given a specific stimulus and no room for options. There is a 100% chance of response x given stimulus y. When Pavlov's dogs were presented with food, there was only one option: salivate.

[14] Past experience is the schedules of reinforcement and current conditions are the antecedent conditions and motivating factors. This, of course, is all allowed for and constrained by biology, or contingencies of survival. Again, this is the philosophy of RB.

they will choose option A about 80 times. However, and this is where the uncertainty comes in, we cannot say exactly in which trials out of the 100 they will choose option A.

Now, what determines this probability in the first place? How can we tell if someone actually has an 80% probability of responding to option A? We can do so simply by using an equation that compares schedules of reinforcement![15] Ah, and it all comes back full circle. This quantitative analysis of choice behavior is called the **matching law**, and it states that *the proportion of responses allocated to an alternative will match the proportion of reinforcement obtained from that alternative* (4). In other words, the matching law predicts how much behavior will be allocated to each option, based on the schedule of reinforcement describing each option.

As a refresher, schedules of reinforcement were introduced in the previous chapter as descriptions that describe the nature of consequences, and specifically, how a consequence is delivered. For example, does a pigeon get a food pellet after pecking the button every time? Every 5th peck? The first peck after 30 seconds has passed since the last peck? Basically, the schedule describes the prerequisites, the necessary response criteria, before reinforcement is delivered.

For example, when reinforcement is received after every five pecks of the blue button, we describe this as a Fixed Ratio 5 schedule. It is fixed because reinforcement is received after a set

---

15 This is surprising, right? You probably didn't think psychologists would have developed a literal formula for understanding behavior, but think again. This is my favorite fun fact to share about behavior analysis.

number of responses, a ratio because reinforcement is contingent upon the number of responses rather than the passage of time, and "5" indicates that reinforcement is received after every five responses. Furthermore, when reinforcement is received after every peck of the red button, we describe it as a Fixed-Ratio 1 schedule. Again, the 1 indicates that reinforcement is received after every response, and "fixed-ratio" means that there is a set number of responses needed. Whether it is fixed or varied, ratio or interval, 1 or 5, constitutes what I describe as the prerequisite; it is just a description of when the reinforcement is delivered. Thus, depending on the history of reinforcement, each available option comes with its own unique schedule of reinforcement, which determines the probability of the behavior occurring.

Okay, I've talked a hot game about being able to precisely calculate the probability, or proportionate rate, of responding, but I have yet to actually give an example. So, let's do it for our pigeon stuck with the blue and red buttons with FR5 and FR1 schedules, respectively. The equation for the matching law is as follows:

$$\frac{B1}{(B1+B2)} = \frac{R1}{(R1+R2)}$$

[16]

where B = behavior (the relative response rate), R = the relative reinforcement rate, 1 = option #1 (red

---

[16] Note that rate implies count/time (e.g., responses per minute or reinforcers per minute).

button), and 2 = option #2 (blue button). All this equation says is that if you divide the number of responses dedicated to option 1 by the total responses dedicated to every option, it will equal the amount of reinforcement provided by that option divided by all total reinforcement provided by every option. In other words, the relative rate of response is proportional to the relative rate of reinforcement. If the left side of the equation (showing the response rate) comes out to 80%, the right side of the equation (showing the reinforcement rate) will come out to 80% as well.[17] Basically, all the matching law says is that when 80% of the total reinforcement is provided by a certain option, we can expect to see 80% of responses dedicated to that certain option.

Now that we have this equation, where do we start? Well, since we are just given information about the schedules of reinforcement (FR5 and FR1), we only have information to fill in the right side of the equation (as this is the side measuring the relative rate of reinforcement). First, let's form an assumption of how many trials are run (i.e., how many instances either button is pushed). Let's say that we observe the pigeon peck a total of 10 times, thus 10 trials. Now, for the first block of 10 trials, let's say that there is an equal response between both options. There are five pecks at blue and five pecks at red because the pigeon is not yet familiar with either of the two keys and has not developed a history of reinforcement with either option. Due to this lack of a relationship with either option,

---

[17] Unless there is bias, which is a concept I will get to in a moment.

responding is like flipping a coin (50/50) until a history of responding has been built up.

Now, after those first 10 responses have transpired and the dust has settled, the red key provided five instances of reinforcement (since it is on an FR1), while the blue key provided only one instance of reinforcement (since it is on an FR5). The red key provided five instances of reinforcement because it only took one peck to prompt the reinforcer, whereas the blue key provided only one instance of reinforcement because it took exactly five pecks on the blue key to receive that reinforcer. Thus, after 10 trials, the pigeon received five reinforcers from pecking the red button and only one reinforcer from pecking the blue button.

Now, we can start plugging in numbers to the equation. For the red button, we get something that looks like this: 5 / (5 + 1) = 5 / 6 = .8333 x 100 = 83.33%. For the blue button we get the following: 1 / (1 + 5) = 1 / 6 = .1666 x 100 = 16.66%. [18] What story do these numbers tell? From the above, we know that because the red button has a relative reinforcement rate of 83.33%, the pigeon will respond 83.33% of the time to the red button. [19] Furthermore, because the blue button has a relative reinforcement rate of 16.66%, we can expect a

---

[18] After the decimal value is determined, we multiply the value by 100 to obtain the percent value.

[19] This assumes, again, that there is no bias. This, again, is a topic I will come to shortly.

response to the blue button 16.66% of the time.[20] Therefore, given another 100 trials, we can expect to see the pigeon peck the red button about 83% of the time and the blue button 17% of the time. However, and here's the nuance, we cannot say in which trials of the 100 the pigeon will choose the red or blue button, nor can we predict exactly how many times the pigeon will pick either key. All we can do is describe the probability with which either option is to be selected and the ratio of responses between options. In other words—getting back to the definition of choice—we can only identify the distribution of operant behavior between options. With this, I humbly acknowledge some limits of our current explanation of behavior-- which should not be a surprise. Yet, let us not make the same mistake as Descartes and assume free will is responsible for that which we cannot yet explain.

However, what if an individual's choice does not reflect what the matching law has predicted? For example, what if the pigeon pecks the red button 90% of the time and the blue button only 10%? What does the current state of behavior analysis say about when the matching law seems "wrong?" Might this be where evidence of free will creeps into view? As you might expect, I and RB adherents alike argue no.

First, as usual, let's start with a definition. When an individual chooses one option *more often* than the matching law predicts, their behavior is said to be **biased** or have a tendency or preference (5). In this case, because the pigeon pecked the red button

---

[20] Notice how the total reinforcement rate between both options adds up to 100%.

more than the matching law predicted (90% instead of 83%), there is bias. Once again, however, this behavior analytic term has a much different meaning in the field than it does colloquially. Bias can better be thought of as unaccounted-for variables, or the conditions we are not aware of. I'll let William Baum, Professor Emeritus at the University of New Hampshire and a figurehead in behavior analysis, clarify bias.

> Bias means unaccounted for preference. It indicates that some independent variable affecting preference hasn't been measured. If all the independent variables were measured and incorporated into the expression estimating reinforcement, there would be no bias. Bias, therefore, reflects no fault on the part of the organism, but only the experimenter's inability to measure or control all the independent variables. (6)

Basically, bias occurs when the observer does not see the whole picture. Thus, bias is not a deviation from the matching law because of the individual's "free will" but instead simply shows an ignorance on the part of the observer. This lack of understanding on the observer's part is also why individuals themselves feel as if they are acting of their own volition. Even when an individual is the observer of their own behavior, they may not be aware of all factors influencing their behavior. This is why if anyone has ever asked you why you are doing something, you may honestly respond by saying, "I don't know." This should be a reminder of a key aspect of RB: one does not have to be aware of the contingencies affecting their behavior to be affected by them. Organisms are always under the control of contingencies, even if they are not aware of those contingencies.

Voluntary and Involuntary

Let's recap everything up to this point. Behaviors that have historically been attributed to free will, inner spirits, or ghosts can be explained in terms of the contingencies of survival and reinforcement. Every response of the organism is in the context of the environment, never operating independently from the rest of nature. Complex operant responding is never certain but is instead analyzed in terms of probability, with odds being influenced by past reinforcement and present conditions (such as motivating operations).

Assuming this is all true, [21] it raises the question, is any behavior truly voluntary? Is everything happening on autopilot? Are we all just mindless drones pre-programmed like the newest coffee machine? This is a common concern that is brought up whenever it is said that free will is a fallacy. To answer this question, no. I do not think humans and other animals behave like robots, mindless drones, or household appliances. There is more to it than that. We are humans.

We have gone over biological responses of the organism (e.g., digestions) as being selected by a process described by Charles Darwin's theory of evolution. There is no evidence of species

---

[21] We are assuming, that is, that this is true for the purpose of this book. But I want my colleagues to work diligently to prove every assumption wrong in the hope that their critical pursuit creates more conclusive evidence supporting RB claims.

determining their biological destiny; rather, biology is selected by the environment. We have gone over reflexes (e.g., salivating) as stimulus-response relationships that can be manipulated through Pavlov's respondent conditioning. These are only possible because of that organism being placed in a species that has evolved the biology that permits certain behaviors. Finally, we have gone over operant behavior (e.g., pecking a red button) as being selected by a process described by Skinner's operant conditioning. These three facets of behavior fall under the giant umbrella of radical behaviorism. Never once did the idea that the organism responds due to its own volition play a role in any of these explanations of behavior.

Thus, through an RB lens, under current definitions we cannot call any behavior "voluntary" if every response can be understood by analyzing the biology of the organism and the environment in which the response takes place. I will repeat, we must not make the same error that Descartes and Galen made; we must not let a current lack of understanding cloud our judgment with the free will fallacy. We must recognize that behavior is not stored in or generated by an organism. Rather, we must operate under the assumption that behavior is an expression of nature nurturing itself, never separate, never distinct, never isolated. Humans, like the air and trees, are part of one endless stream of existence, never separate in action.

There needs to be a new conceptualization of what it means to be an individual, radically changing the idea of the "self." The self is not something overshadowing an individual like an aura but the repertoire of behavior they have developed over their lifetime. An individual is a culmination of experience, the manifestation of unique genetics in a unique environment. They are something indistinguishable from nature, being deeply intertwined with all else. Nothing voluntary or involuntary—just nature proceeding as it is.

Forgiveness and Punishment

Imagine that tomorrow, everyone everywhere accepts the idea that free will is bunk. That people do not act because of their own volition or soul but because of reasons so complex we still do not fully understand them. What next? What kinds of repercussions should this create? What are the implications of a lack of free will?

One of the first topics of discussion that comes up is the idea of forgiveness. Should everyone be constantly forgiven, exonerated, or absolved of accountability for their past mistakes, as vile as they may be? In other words, what are we to do about criminals? Should murder, rape, violence, theft, burglary, tax evasion, child predation, slavery, sex trafficking, and drunk driving all be accepted and made legal? Should governments not hold their citizens to any proper standards of decency or law? Should there be no legal system, no establishment of justice, no jail or prison, no accountability for one's harmful actions? Should criminals walk the street forever to ravage the safety of citizens?

Absolutely not. These are the easiest implications to dispense with. As Sapolsky said when talking about this very same idea, "People must be protected from individuals who are dangerous," something that most, if not all, readers will agree on (7). To use Sapolsky's example, nobody wants a car to be hurtling down the road with its brakes cut because this is extremely dangerous and will likely cause destruction. Yet, the fact that there is a reason the car is hurling down the street uncontrollably (e.g., a brake malfunction) does not mean people are okay with it or that it is not an issue of concern. Just as we do not want a car running lose, speeding out of control, we do not want murderers and rapists out on the hunt, prowling the streets, abducting our children, and preying on the innocent. Thus, just because there is a reason, an explanation other than free will, for why someone murders, steals, and rapes, this does not mean that their behavior should be accepted or permitted. Even with "good" and "bad" being subjective, a self-governed citizenry will identify behaviors that they either disapprove or approve of and want to eradicate or promote (punish or reinforce). A self-governing population will decide the subjectivity of good and bad and enforce laws appropriately — this is simply the nature of culture. For America, this explains our cultural disapproval of violence and dishonesty, which is reflected in harsh prison sentences for murder, tax fraud, and other acts of this kind.[22] This is simply something our culture has come to prefer.

Now, if a lack of free will does not mean excusing bad behaviors, then what does it mean? Well, a lack of free will means that we must recognize some behaviors as bad without blaming

---

[22] Still, everything happens in context. This means that even though most Americans think killing someone is bad, many can also justify killing someone given a particular context, such as it being in self-defense. In this case, being the aggressor is unacceptable, while being the defender is acceptable. Of course, things are never so cut-and-dried; it always depends on the context.

that bad behavior solely on the individual, as if they are inherently a bad person or their bad behavior originated from within them. No free will means that we still recognize that a person does something wrong but not that the "soul" of that person is to blame or is corrupt. Under this predicate, there is no room for the idea that punishment is righteous or that *a person* "deserves" to be punished. After all, if a person is not freely behaving because of some inner "self," then trying to tear down that evil inner "self" with harsh prison sentences will not do anything because there is no inner 'self' to change![23] There is only behavior to change.

By no longer attributing behavior ('good' or 'bad') to free will, we can no longer blame the person for their actions or cast them away as if they are a bad person with a horrible rotten soul. There becomes no logical way to place blame on the person if it is assumed that their bad behavior did not originate from within them but is instead a product of contingencies of reinforcement

---

[23] In operant conditioning, we do not punish (or reinforce) the *person*, we punish their *behavior*. So right off the bat, to say that we should punish the person means nothing to a behavior analyst. Furthermore, even if we do decide to use punishment when people commit crimes, we must make sure that the punishment procedure actually works, which currently, it arguably does not. A prison sentence is not abrupt, immediate, brief, or similar to the natural consequences of their actions, nor do the targeted behaviors always decrease in response. Thus, by definition, it is hard to call prison a system of punishment for those who get stuck in its cycle.

constrained and allowed for by contingencies of survival — which, after all, is the whole assumption of RB. However, if we insist on pointing fingers and assigning blame like wrathful children, the only thing we can point to is the biology of that person and their history in the environment. Both are out of the control of the individual. And at that point, what's the point of even getting all worked up about blaming something anyway? Though fun, the blame game is no longer the game we adults should be playing; let's give up this idea of blame and switch to one of nurturance and growth.

Therefore, we must manufacture a different approach to dealing with convicts: not one that places blame and indignation on the individual but one that recognizes the roots of behavior and how to foster the growth of new behavior. This approach should both decrease the frequency of problem behaviors and increase the frequency of culturally appropriate behaviors. That should be the main, if not only, goal. It would represent a complete renaissance in how we think of criminals and what we do with them.

Luckily, the current state of behavior analysis tells us exactly how to do this. We can selectively decrease certain behaviors while increasing others with a little procedure called **differential reinforcement.** [24] And — here's the kicker — it does

---

[24] Differential reinforcement is the process of reinforcing a specific response in a particular context and not reinforcing (i.e., extinguishing) other responses. More specifically, it involves providing either positive or negative reinforcement for a targeted response (or targeted member of a response class) and withholding reinforcement from all other responses (or members of a response class). The withholding of reinforcement is defined as "extinction." Thus, differential

not use punishment. Imagine a future where, instead of prison being an aversive environment designed to degrade and humiliate the prisoners, who are treated like rats, it is instead something akin to a school where prisoners are modeled into responsible and productive citizens. In a sense, making the weakest links in our chains stronger. This would be a system that does not solely rely on "punishment" but instead incorporates a fuller understanding of behavior into policies and procedures that work for all individuals sent through those prison halls.

As interesting as this topic is, and as much as I want to talk about my ideas of how to change the prison system, that is not the point here. The point I make with this section and chapter is that just because behavior can be explained by reasons outside of the individual's control does not make that behavior "okay." What makes that behavior acceptable is the culture and context in which that behavior happens. Furthermore, we must stop looking at the person themselves as "bad," evil, wicked, or immoral and instead see their behavior as such. There needs to be a simple shift in language that describes the behavior as "bad," not the person. This is not a removal of blame but a shift in blame— from the individual to the environment and biology. If we stop looking at the person as "bad" and instead just look at their behaviors that way, we can form a different relationship with that person. Rather than looking down upon a person and seeing them as all that is disgusting and wrong with the world, we can see them as a unique individual worthy of having their perspective

---

reinforcement is a two-part process: reinforcing the desired response(s) and extinguishing all other responses (8).

recognized. This is an important idea to remember throughout the second half of this book.

Part Two:
Application

Chapter V

Our Shared Goal

"Freedom. Justice. Opportunity. Throughout the history of nations, the freedom to think, speak, write, and create; to possess diverse political, social, and religious views; to own and use property and produce and distribute goods and services, has rarely existed. What has made all of these freedoms a permanent part of our nation is the Constitution. Two hundred years ago, a document was written that would bring tens of millions of people to our shores to seek a new life... to pursue hopes and goals unheard of and unattainable anywhere else in the world... This historic occasion gives all of us a chance to pay tribute to a way of life that guarantees every man and woman the freedom and opportunity necessary to achieve success. It wouldn't be America if we didn't all share this belief in the critical importance of the individual... if we couldn't, through hard work and determination, turn our own dreams of happiness and success into reality." (1)

- Richard S. Braddock

....

In the first part of this book, I discussed how individuals' distinct genetics and novel environments have made everyone the unique individuals they are. Every manifestation of the individual is catered by nature while also being constantly tinkered with by the environment.[25] It has been my goal to ingrain this in the reader's mind. Brain architecture, neural and hormonal flux, and the most seemingly profound or personal day-to-day choices one makes all showcase the enormous variability in behavior among people. If you thought those beautiful snowflakes falling from the sky in winter were unique... oh boy, do they pale in comparison to humans.

In the second part of this book, I will discuss how to apply RB's recognition of individual uniqueness to foster cooperation (and downright human decency) in a political context, such as during policy or program discourse between anyone, from friends and family to heads of state.[26] Let us have no more ruined Thanksgivings because aunts and cousins are at each other's throats with the turkey carver about some controversial policy; fewer friendships tarnished because of differences in political party affiliation; fewer posts on social media directing hate and showing disgust toward

---

[25] "Catering" and "tinkering" are good substitutes for contingencies of survival and contingencies of reinforcement.

[26] I prefer to say "policy discourse" instead of "policy debate" because in debate, there is a winner and a loser, whereas discourse can lead to compromise. The difference in connotation is to have a discussion rather than a battle, or to work together instead of trying to defeat the "other."

everyone who voted for the "other" candidate. Simply put, how do we help people just get along? That is the goal.

More specifically, the goal is to dissolve this 'us/them' behavior we see that is responsible for such animosity between our own people. [27] We want to do away with the idea of seeing someone who is different from you politically, in even just one way, as some foreign, disgusting scum of the earth and acting as if that is so, with all the dehumanizing repercussions that come with it. This rests on separation and distinction, removal and division, the drawing of arbitrary lines between people because of some "immoral" opinion or characteristic you perceive or assume them to have. Seeing the "other" or "them" as if they are less than human is like a disease festering in the population that needs to be eradicated or like barnacles leaching onto the bottom of the boat that need to be scraped off. In this latter part of the book, I will talk about how to get rid of this dangerous overgeneralization by showing how we can use our modern understanding of behavior to motivate more inclusive "us" behavior with less "them-ing" behavior. This will teach the reader how to behave more as a friend than a foe, even in times when they may find this most difficult. It will allow us to see people as the unique individuals they are instead of as the disgusting manifestations of all things that

-----

[27] This book is written primarily for an American audience, so when I say things such as "us," "our," or "we," I am referring to Americans, specifically those who vote and are engaged in political discourse. However, the message can be extended to a global or international scope by seeing everyone, together, as part of one human species.

are horrible with a group you associate them with. The rest of this book will be about how to apply what we have learned about human behavior to easing the apparent political divide that is making people see more and more Americans as disgusting "others." This, then, is the turning point in the book where I zoom out from just talking about psychology and philosophy and finally get into how we can actually make our society better!

The Origins of Us and Them

To this day, my favorite baseball team is the Boston Red Sox. To answer the reader's first question, neither I nor any of my family come from Boston. I think the love for the team can be traced back to a youth summer camp where a pretty counselor was wearing a Boston hat. Not family tradition, not love for specific players, but something completely unrelated—a pretty girl. Pair a pretty girl with a neutral baseball team and, just like that, out comes a lifelong fan. After all, marketing companies know, sex sells for a reason. Interestingly enough, with that newfound love for the Red Sox also came some negative feelings toward, you guessed it, the New York Yankees. Though as an adult, I have grown out of this behavior, as a child, I thought all Yankees players and fans were rotten, mean jerks.[28] All I knew was that the Red Sox and Yankees were rivals, which meant that they didn't like each other, which meant I didn't like the Yankees or, by extension, any of their fans and players. I began to form a certain negative relationship with

---

[28] Sorry, Yankees fans.

everything Yankee, everything that could be related to the Yankees became aversive. [29] Of course, after growing up, I realized that this sports rivalry is not so deep that it should affect who I choose to make my friend. Most importantly, I learned that simply being a Yankees fan does not make someone dirt. The moral of the story is that I stopped overgeneralizing and started seeing the individual under the team jersey.

In my example about the Red Sox and Yankees, I illustrated that this divisive 'us/them' behavior can happen with something as simple as sports teams and a pretty girl. Now, what happens when there is this division in a political context — say, between a Democrat and a Republican? Here comes the challenging part: dissolving these seemingly rigid barriers that divide people. I'll be the first to say it: making people realize that they are on the same team can be incredibly difficult, especially when there just seems to be no middle ground, as in the debate between someone being pro-life and pro-choice. I have heard the same thing from people on both sides, "there just is no middle ground.". Furthermore, breaking up this harmful dichotomy seems especially difficult because, after all, these distinctions and groupings of others happen automatically, without conscious awareness, and out of the control of the individual. [30] Think of the Red Sox example: my behavior of liking the Red Sox was selected by my

---

[29] I admit this is a limited diagnostic of the situation, there are unique aspects of human language involved which I will not discuss but are described by Steven Hayes theory on human language and higher cognition, RFT.

[30] This is the point I was trying to hammer down in the first part of the book.

environment, not some inner urge to fulfill a personal desire. Just like all other behaviors, it is not because of the individual's own free will that they behave this way but rather because of the biological-environmental relationships specific to the individual and generalized over the species.

For example, humans are biologically predisposed to activate their amygdala (center for emotions and fear) rather than their fusiform face area (center for recognizing faces) in the first short (as in 50 milliseconds) exposure of looking at someone of another race.[31] As the reader might be able to guess, this activation pattern is more intense in someone who is racist (2). Thus, from a neuroscience and behavioral point of view, for those first few milliseconds of interaction, someone of race A is behaving as if someone of race B is not a human.[32] This is degradation to the highest degree. I feel a cold chill wash over me with that fact: there is "us/theming" right from the start.

Now we are left with two major, interesting tidbits of insight from this. First, this divisive grouping behavior into "us and them" is biologically pre-programmed and happens as a reflex (at least with those of other races). Second, this response can either increase or decrease

---

[31] This makes sense evolutionarily because it is relatively recently in human history that people ever saw someone who was in such a different culture that they had a different skin color. However, this is just speculation.

[32] This basic ability most likely plays a significant role in dehumanization, which is the viewing of someone as if they are something less than human. This is also the case for racist calls for genocide, which usually refer to the target group as less than human, diseases, insects, parasites.

depending upon the individual's history with the environment, i.e., through respondent conditioning. Just as Pavlov's dog learned to salivate after hearing the bell, people can learn to cringe in disgust at people of a certain group through stimulus pairings in the environment. This can even be something as innocent as a satisfying smell, annoying sound, foul taste, or pretty girl wearing a Boston hat.[33] For instance, if, every day, when someone walks past a movie theater, they are hit with a whiff of rotten sewer stench, they could learn to pair that movie theater with that disgusting sewer smell. Thus, the endless pairing of stimuli and relationship building begins. Not only does the movie theater get paired, or related, with that aversive smell, but so do the people who go to that theater, the workers and management there, and the movies they play; this basic accounts for how this relationship of stimuli spreads like wildfire.[34]

Thankfully, with exception to the racists, after a little more time passes and the environment settles in, their history of reinforcement catches up with them, and they start to behave as if they are indeed looking at another human. [35] This brings us to another protagonist of the book: operant conditioning. Not only does operant conditioning

---

[33] Here's something to think about: this might be the insight as to why people say things such as, "I don't know why I don't like them; they just leave a bad taste in my mouth."

[34] Please note that there is much to it than this, like the involvement of our unique human language capabilities, described by Steven Hayes' RFT.

[35] For the racist, it is also their history that is responsible for their exaggerated amygdala activation and the continual disgust that follows.

play a role in creating this divisive behavior, but it is also the key to stopping it. Talk about a double-edged sword!

Let's talk first about how operant conditioning contributes to this "us/them-ing." Behavior can be conditioned so that responses described as divisive, hateful, and discriminatory all either increase or decrease in probability. For example, we can identify any behavior, or belief, that can be called racist by finding the trail of reinforcement that has been increasing and maintaining that behavior. This is basic reinforcement. Examine a typical racist behavior, such as calling someone a slur (I'll leave the exact one up to the reader's imagination). The first question is, where did this word come from? This can be better said as, why did this person have this word in their repertoire? Where did they learn it from? Well, most likely, they learned whichever word the reader is thinking of because they heard someone else say it, or they accidentally said it once before and afterward experienced reinforcing consequences. This seems pretty simple.[36] Calling someone a slur has been socially reinforced; saying that slur is a behavior that has been selected by the social environment one is surrounded by. This is pretty much the same story for how all other language and social behavior is learned— mediation by those in your sphere of influence.[37]

---

[36] Again, I am leaving out the entire conversation of the involvement of language described by Steven Hayes' RFT.

[37] Furthermore, there are sometimes even established rules that command people to divide and discriminate. The historic American example of this is Jim Crow-era segregation of whites and blacks, even for things as innocent as water fountains.

However, the reality is more nuanced than that, as it usually is. One's racist behavior depends on the context at the moment the choice is available to say the slur. For instance, many people will let loose and say all kinds of things in the privacy of their homes with their friends but will not even come close to saying such things in public or around their parents. For these people, being in public or with certain family members is not an appropriate context in which to use such slurs. For people in this scenario, the tendency to use a racial slur has only been reinforced in the context of their friends and punished or extinguished in almost every other social context. They understand that there may be a time and a place for saying this word, but "that time is not now, and that place is not here." This should not be a surprise. After all, it's with friends that one is supposed to be able to let loose and behave in ways that are otherwise not accepted by others. That's the whole idea behind what makes certain people friends: being able to do things that we otherwise would not feel comfortable doing because such things have either been punished or extinguished by others while being reinforced by one's friends. Having these shared contingencies tightly binding us around similar experiences and being aware of those bonds makes us behave precisely as an "us".

This is a perfect segue into how we can use an understanding of this "us/them-ing" behavior to start behaving as a friendly "us". We can do so by figuring out what we have in common—figuring out what unites us instead of divides us. We must recognize the common thread that weaves all of us together in the conga line of a dance that is life. We must realize that we are all on the same boat and that we all need to row the paddles.

America's Superordinate Goal

The first step in breaking down this "us/them-ing" behavior (and starting to cooperate) is finding the common ground, or the superordinate, otherwise known as shared, goal. Why is this shared goal so important? Well, when we are behaving as if someone else is a "them," we behave as if "we" have nothing in common with "them." We act as if "they" are all that is wrong with the world, thus dehumanizing "them" and letting their individual uniqueness fade into the shadow of some group. Thus, it's very difficult to get people to have effective communication when some people think they are so different from the others that there is no middle ground. We cannot get wrapped up in this kind of thinking; it is a trap! There is a middle ground, especially in American politics.

What does a superordinate goal do that is so important for dissolving this "us/them" behavior? Establishing a superordinate goal creates a shared contingency — roughly, something everyone can unite around. It is something that everyone is working toward and cares deeply about. Finding and being reminded of, or primed for, what people have in common shifts their behavior from "them" to "us" (3). A superordinate goal acts as an antecedent intervention to get people to behave more with respect to their similarities with others rather than their differences, i.e., as "us." This goal shifts the focus from what makes us different to what makes us similar.

Red Sox fans of all shapes and sizes put differences aside and enjoy a few hours together watching their team hit homers over the Green Monster. Friends of all backgrounds come together around their shared interests to let loose and can "be themselves." A superordinate goal reveals one thing or idea that all parties (in this case, political parties) have in common. For Americans, regardless of race, religion, economic status, health, politics, sex, or gender, we are fortunate to have the ideas so beautifully written in the Constitution to unite around[38]. Regardless of political party, these are the ideals we all have in common. This is not just my opinion; this is quite literally the purpose of the preamble to the Constitution: to serve as the superordinate goal for this country. It is something

---

[38] This is a point I know will come up, so I must address it. Some readers might question this and say that America has never lived up to its promises, and that this document and country has only ever been for white men. After all, there was a time of slavery, Jim Crow, redlining, and other discriminatory acts denying black Americans their freedoms (there has been other mistreatment, but I will use this as an example). And to that I say, you are correct only insofar as we have not lived up to our ideals; humans are not perfect, and there will always be people trying to take away the freedom of others. However, this is exactly why our Constitution was written—because humans are not perfect and there will always be those trying to enslave and degrade others. I agree that it is a problem that we do not live up to the ideals set in the Constitution, but those goals are still powerfully liberating and are shared by the overwhelming majority of Americans. So, no, we have not always lived up to our ideals, but we are constantly working towards doing so. Dr. Martin Luther King did not ask for new rights, he only ever asked for the ones he, and every American, were granted from birth. We can all agree that these ideals set forth are desirable, and we can also agree that we have not always accomplished those goals. These ideas are not mutually exclusive.

that unites, not divides. Having trouble remembering it? Here, let me help jog your memory.

The preamble to the Constitution states, "*We the People of the United States, in Order to form a more perfect Union, establish Justice, insure domestic Tranquility, provide for the common defense, promote the general Welfare, and secure the Blessings of Liberty to ourselves and our Posterity...*" (4). The superordinate goal for all Americans is to form a more perfect union by achieving five fundamental principles: establishing justice, ensuring domestic tranquility, providing for the common defense, promoting the general welfare, and securing the blessings of liberty to ourselves and our posterity. It is difficult to find any other political doctrine more unifying, or direct, than this. This sentence is, by definition, a superordinate goal. Not only does the preamble state exactly what to do, but that we, the people, all of us excluding none, have the power and duty to accomplish this task. This is not just a task for a certain faction of the country, or people who voted for a certain candidate, but rather the task of our citizenry as a whole. All citizens, regardless of race, religion, sex, sexual orientation, or economic status, have a role in creating a more perfect union. Accomplishing this goal is not a partisan or controversial task; this is a fundamental principle of America, our superordinate goal that facilitates cooperation; this is what makes us "US."

We are not as divided as the media may make it seem. Any normal distribution will tell us that, though there are political actors at both extremes, most Americans rest in the middle. It is irresponsible to overgeneralize people because of one identifiable characteristic, such as simply voting Democrat or Republican. This point is echoed by former President Obama's remarks at the 2004 Democratic National Convention:

> The pundits like to slice-and-dice our country into red states and blue states: red states for Republicans, Blue states for Democrats. But I've got news for them, too. We worship an awesome God in the blue states, and we don't like federal agents poking around in our libraries in the red states. We coach little league in the blue states and, yes, we've got some gay friends in the red states. There are patriots who opposed the war in Iraq, and patriots who supported the war in Iraq. (5)

A Problem Remains

We have established a superordinate goal: fulfilling the values of the preamble to the Constitution. We can start to see all Americans not as divided into segregated groups but as one people. However, is that all we must do? Unfortunately, it's not. A major difficulty still rests ahead. That we have identified a common goal does not mean that the world becomes one big hippie love fest full of sunshine and daisies. Red Sox fans still get into drunken fights with each other, friends still argue about petty things and end relationships, and Americans are still left with vastly different ideas as to how those goals in the preamble should best be achieved. There will always be disagreement, argument, debate, but hopefully, mature discussion and emotional regulation prevails.

Imagine being on a road trip with your best friend. The destination has been decided: the goal is to get to Lake Tahoe and enjoy the beautiful blue water and pristine pine trees. You and your friend are in the same car and are going to the same place. The only problem is that you and your friend have different routes you want to take to get there. You have your reasons for why you want to go your way, and your friend has an equally dense list of reasons for why you should go their way. Though you and your friend have the destination picked out, the route to get there is still discussed. This is the same thing that is happening in American politics — just at a much higher level of magnitude of complexity and consequence.

Now that we have gotten rid of this idea of other Americans being absolute 'them-s' (at least in a political context), we can start to illuminate the individual uniqueness that has been hidden for so long by the overcast of the group. Now that there is a base value we can be primed with to make us behave as "us," we must see everyone as the unique individual they are. We must individuate. We must take the perspective of each unique individual. We must find out why people behave (e.g., believe) as they do by attributing that behavior's origin not to some mysterious inner self but rather to the contingencies of reinforcement and survival. We must approach these difficult conversations with tolerance for others.[39] We must be curious to understanding others.

---

[39] Tolerance extends only up to a collectively determined extent (i.e., within the scope of the law).

Chapter VI

Our Individual Goals

"Practice perspective taking, individuate, individuate, individuate." (1)

- Robert Sapolsky

....

We have established the superordinate goal for all Americans — fulfilling the Preamble to the Constitution. However, that is not enough to render everything free from political argument and rid the world of negative emotions. There are still issues that people do not see eye-to-eye on, divergent philosophies, and vastly different opinions. Or, said more behaviorally with a spice of imagery, there are still conflicting contingencies ramming into each other like clashing bulls. But most of all, people still see others as disgusting monsters for these differences in perceptions, opinions, and beliefs. [40] This division is a grave problem that needs to be addressed. So, what must we do about this continued animosity and debate? After all, there will always be differences in opinion; the only question concerns what to do about those differences.[41]

It's simple. We must learn to value and appreciate each other's uniqueness.[42] How so, you might ask? Well, we do it by first recognizing everyone's uniqueness as valuable and then taking their perspective. It's a short, two-step process with mountains of empirical evidence behind it. Still, this is easier said than done. Just like any behavior, the skills of individuating and perspective taking require time to become proficient at. Even after the skills are learned, the environment still needs to be such that that individuals actually execute these skills (i.e., there must be proper antecedent conditions and motivating operants). Now, I cannot make anyone learn these skills. However, I can use this book as an antecedent intervention to motivate such behavior for those who are capable—which should very well be every reader. That is the goal.

Nonetheless, to further break down any remaining "us/ them-ing" and have any hope of cooperating, we must practice perspective taking (2). This is the way to stop all this division and attain some well-needed political ease. By behaving

---

[40] If your blood curdles when learning that someone is or isn't a "whatever" supporter, that is what I am talking about.

[41] Thanks to individual uniqueness, there is never a shortage of new and different opinions.

[42] In a political context, of course. I have already noted that things of law, such as murder, rape, pedophilia, are not tolerated, and what is intolerable is decided by the culture.

with curiosity to learn about those with differing opinions,[43] we can talk about our different road maps in a way without being at each other's throats—a way that appreciates and values different perspectives. Thus, it is my belief that all individuals who choose to participate in discourse with the hope of achieving cooperation have the responsibility to take other perspectives.

Your Brain on Perspective Taking

Alright, let's slow down a bit. I am talking a big game about perspective taking, how it can break down "us/them" behavior as well as strengthen conversation and help compromise. But why does it work so beautifully (or at least have the potential to act so well)? Well, let's start with a definition. Perspective taking is defined by the APA as looking at a situation from a viewpoint that is different from one's usual viewpoint (3). Roughly, this means walking a mile in another person's shoes, putting yourself in another's position, exerting effort to see the world through the eyes of another.[44] In effect, perspective taking is behaving as if you were someone else. Now, why does behaving as if you were someone else (i.e., role-playing) help build tolerance? To understand this, it will be helpful to introduce a little neuroscience.

---

[43] This curiosity to learn about different beliefs is line with the value of education I have repeated through this book,

[44] Interesting fact: perspective taking, and other theory of mind activities can be quite challenging for those on the autism spectrum. Even cooler fact: ABA can help kids with autism learn these complex social skills.

Perspective taking has been shown to be correlated with certain brain activities that are involved in emotional control and decision-making. Colloquially, this activation can be thought of as not letting your emotions get the best of you and thinking before you act. [45] This increase in activation occurs specifically in the ventromedial prefrontal cortex (vmPFC) and the dorsal medial prefrontal cortex (dmPFC), with a decrease in activation of the amygdala. (4)[46] The vmPFC and dmPFC are areas of the squishy pink outer layer of the brain most commonly thought of as "the brain," located in the most front part of the brain, while the amygdala is housed deeper in the brain and is said to be the emotional center of the brain. Connect the dots, and we see that activation in the vmPFC is correlated with the inhibition of conditioned emotional responses (6). This makes sense because amygdala activation is correlated with emotional response. Thus, a decrease in amygdala activation also means a decrease in emotional response.[47] Said

---

[45] These are things we have hopefully all heard since childhood.

[46] However, as Sapolsky said in his book *Behave*, "Like everything about the brain, the structure and function of the frontal cortex vary enormously among individuals..." (5). This again highlights the uniqueness of the individual due to their environmental history and genetics.

[47] Activations of these areas are not the causes of any behavior. Rather, the activations of these areas can themselves be thought of as behaviors—the first responses of the organism in a chain of responding that eventually reveals itself as overt, or observable, behavior. After all, these brain regions do not activate randomly. Something happens in the environment, and the organism responds according to its

more behaviorally, learned emotional reactions, such as anger, sadness, and frustration, are incompatible with perspective taking. This is big news! This means that, when you are taking a perspective, you are less likely to be irritable and less likely to associate that person with all the disgusting evils of the world you have been conditioned to associate them with. This is the key component of staying calm and mature in the presence of adversity, specifically the speech and opinions of others. Not only will diverse ideas now spread to those previously least willing to hear such perspectives; those same people will become less hostile. Finally, we have a credible solution to animosity.

The Value of Perspective Taking

As the conversation pivots, I can think of no better example for illustrating the value of perspective taking than the Hindu parable of the seven blind men and the elephant. It perfectly depicts why input from other group members is so valuable for cooperation and why we must tolerate others' opinions and speech. For those who have never heard this story, it goes something like this.

There are seven blind men tasked with identifying an elephant, but each man touches only a distinct part of the elephant that the others do not touch. This makes it so that the men have a limited awareness of the environment, even more so than their blindness constraining them. As a result of

---

history with such environments as well as its genetic constraints.

touching different parts of the elephant, they all claim that what they are touching is something unique (i.e., that they have the answer). The first man touched the trunk and declared the elephant to be a large snake. Another man reached the elephant's ear, which he described as a kind of fan. Man after man touched the elephant but described something different. The man who touched the elephant's leg proclaimed it to be a tree trunk. The man who touched the elephant's side said it was a wall. The one who felt its tail described it as a rope, and the man who felt its tusk stated that the elephant is hard, smooth, and spear-like (7). Thus, none of the men alone are fully aware of the environment as it truly manifests itself. All men are ignorant, and nobody is omniscient.

Now, and this is me veering off from the original story, let's say the men begin to converse about their experiences (without touching other parts of the elephant, just talking with the other men) with the goal of discovering what it is that they have encountered. This is the superordinate goal that the previous chapter invokes. However, imagine further that the man who believed the trunk to be a snake, let's call him Jerry, is so persistent in his belief that he fights and screams down the other men until they give in and agree to label the entire elephant a snake out of pure exhaustion and fear. Jerry, passionate in his desire to be correct and assert his perception as an unquestionable truth, bulldozes over the other men and leaves their perceptions in the abyss to be forgotten. All of their perceptions are dispensed with as if they are illegitimate.

Ultimately, by being so stubborn and intolerant, resisting acknowledgement of the merits of what the other men have experienced, Jerry is holding everyone back from a more complete understanding of reality. Even though Jerry is confident that his perception is a correct description of the elephant, by silencing and ignoring the valuable perception of others, he is not only limiting his own perception but also the total collective knowledge of his peer group. Jerry's intolerant insistence that his ideas are the only correct ones drags all the other men down and stops progress toward the superordinate goal. Thus, without perspective taking and listening to others, there will be no cooperation toward a superordinate goal, just aggression and resentfulness; there will only be an ignorant assumption that one's perception is correct above all others, ultimately hindering progress in all pursuits.[48]

Needless to say, this intolerant push for one's ideas over all else is not behavior to be modeled. Our culture would call this "bad" behavior or not playing nicely. So let me show you behavior to model, or "good" behavior. Let's again take Jerry, the one who believed the trunk to be a snake, but now imagine him having the skills of perspective taking and tolerance and being in the right environment for that behavior to come to fruition — he just read this book perhaps. This time, unlike before, he approaches the situations with intellectual humility and allows the other men to give their experiential accounts and explanations for why they believe the object to be what it is they

---

[48] This becomes partially true when a person starts trying to assert their moral or ethical philosophy as the one true philosophy everyone must accept, even when there are other beliefs that are just as defensible, if not more so.

believe it to be. Most importantly, he does not become physically violent in his pursuit to change the minds of the other men. He, and all the men alike, simply discuss what they think they know based on unique experiences and are all curious about the experiences of each other.

Before going any further, it is hopefully obvious what a difference in results these two scenarios yield. One is disastrously authoritarian, while the other involves collaboratively transcending. In the latter scenario, Jerry is still confident in his belief, yet he does not discount the experiences of others. By allowing others the opportunity to express their beliefs, he is able to learn a thing or two—or six, to be exact—in this scenario. By expressing his views, he allows others to do the same. The dissemination of ideas among peers is a key result of perspective taking.

The big takeaway? Individuals who lack the learned ability to acknowledge the limitations of their beliefs will only continue to fall victim to their own ignorance and deprive everyone else of enlightenment. However, those who do take different perspectives will forever be humble students alongside their peers, always trying to learn more. This is way holding the values of education and courage is paramount.

One must understand that, because every individual is unique, there are always more contingencies that they have not yet encountered, more parts of the world that they have no relationship with; there is an eternal mystery. Thus, when an individual learns that they do not have all of the answers but need to rely on others for more information, the value of listening to others' perspectives and gaining insight from their experiences increases. It is simple motivation.

Freedom and the Responsibility of Tolerance

Okay, we have an idea as to why perspective taking works and why it is valuable, but why is it necessary? It is because of the existence of freedom. Specifically, I mean that since individuals are given the ability to express themselves freely, there arises the simultaneous responsibility to tolerate others' free expression as well. You cannot have your freedom but be intolerant of others' freedoms; it does not work like that. Because you get your freedom to vary, so does everyone else, and we all must respect that. This is not up for debate.[49]

But why are we talking about freedom, anyway? Well, it's because, in America, the diversity of thought is protected! People have the right to possess different opinions, values, beliefs, and religions; people are allowed to express different opinions politically. Everyone is allowed to vary on their own unique path. Everyone is allowed to have a different idea of how we can best achieve our superordinate goal. And boy, do we.

To come to a compromise and get us closer to fulfilling the goals stated in the Preamble, we must first be able to bear a conversation with those who have different ideals than us—which is basically everyone. We cannot just silence those who disagree with us; their perspectives hold valuable information that we may be overlooking, fruitful information that will better our own perspectives. After all, if everyone has a unique perspective, then

---

[49] Again, I have already noted that there are culturally specific behaviors that have already been solidified as punishable by law.

there are important things you are not aware of that someone else is, and vice versa. That means allowing everyone to say everything that they feel needs to be said – no self-censorship. This is a little something called freedom of speech.[50]

Thus, when we start to take the perspectives of others, we must allow others to be honest in their expressions. That means allowing people to say things that will upset, anger, and even frustrate us. However, this means that the listener bears the responsibility of tolerating whatever speech others may engage in. My reasoning for this claim lies in America's founding documents.

Embedded in America's Declaration of Independence is the philosophy of liberalism, the political and social philosophy that promotes individual rights, civil liberties, democracy, and free enterprise (9). These are all things that allow individual uniqueness to thrive. By affirming that "we hold these truths to be self-evident, that all men are created equal, that they are endowed by their Creator with certain unalienable Rights, that among these are Life, Liberty and the pursuit of Happiness," America vows to protect the freedom of the individual (10). In essence, America tries to make certain that individuals can vary and proceed down their own path of life with limited interference from the government, so long as they do not harm others.

---

[50] The First Amendment states that "Congress shall make no law respecting an establishment of religion, or prohibiting the free exercise thereof; or abridging the freedom of speech, or of the press." Thus, the right of the individual's free expression of belief and thought was safeguarded (8). Freedom of expression protects individual uniqueness.

Now, for this protection of the sovereign individual's rights to manifest in society, a commonly shared axiom of tolerance must be present. [51] This means that an underlying commitment between all citizens to put up with each other up to a collectively determined and justifiable extent is necessary in facilitating the coexistence of differing beliefs. [52] Variability will not flourish if variability is not tolerated. This does not mean that you must love or enjoy every quirky person's offsetting choices all the time. You simply just have to remain calm and not rip their heads off (i.e., not engage in any illegal or violent behavior against someone else). As we say to children, keep your hands to yourself, and play nice.

Recognizing the importance of free and honest self-expression is the common thread that binds a liberal society and permits variability in behavior and belief. This must be a deeply shared contingency among all people. If the rights of others are not recognized, we will start behaving as if we have forgotten their rights, which only brings us back to the divisive "us/them" behavior we were trying to get away from. [53] This section serves as a reminder of these rights, focusing awareness on

---

[51] Though this shared axiom of tolerance is not a superordinate goal, it can be described as the common Way, a concept originating from Sun Tzu's five factors in *The Art of War*.

[52] The culture will determine what constitutes justifiable acts, again showing the context-specificity of it all.

[53] Similarly, if we forget our common goal, we will behave as if we have none. This is simple priming, or antecedent intervention.

what has been right under our noses this whole time. We must let the recognition of individual uniqueness and the protection thereof motivate our tolerant and mature behavior.

The Courage of Perspective Taking and Compromising

If cooperating was as easy as saying my ABCs, there would be no need for me to write this book; we would be living in a wonderful fairytale utopia. Yet, we do not, which is no one's fault on their own. Perspective taking, adapting one's beliefs, letting others speak and listening to provocative opinions, and letting go of some demands so that others can satisfy some of their requests, is all very challenging. By nature, you must do something aversive. That is, something you would rather not have to do. This makes sense, as the ideas counter to your own are presumably have not been reinforced and are either neutral or aversive. Of course, it would be easier to pretend that people with different opinions didn't exist, but life has not granted that luxury. After all, if you were able to always, easily do only whatever you "wanted" (mentalistically), there would be no need for compromise either—you would simply ignore others and retreat into your own comforting familiarity. That's easy. What's hard is facing the ideas that get you riled up emotionally and trying to understand those frightening concepts as if they were your own. That takes courage; that is doing the right thing even when it is the harder thing to do.

It takes immense courage to admit when a previously held belief or idea was wrong or misguided. All too often, people let their happiness depend on the fulfillment of perceptual desire, as in always being correct about everything. This is a possible reason why, for some, admitting fault may be seen as a sign of weakness. On this point, I ask the reader to consider an alternative way of thinking. By recognizing that you are wrong sometimes, you are actually being brave, not weak. Rather than being an admission of defeat and incompetence, it can better be thought of as intellectual fortitude in line with a value of education. Such noble humility is exactly the kind of behavior a leader must exhibit if they have any honest intention of promoting cooperation. Advancing toward uncomfortable, opposing perspectives, adapting beliefs and behavior to new credible perspectives, or even forfeiting some of our own deeply held beliefs so the ideals of others can go recognized and become incorporated—that is gallant and is the precise behavior that leads to a successful culture.

In fact, this advancement toward the uncomfortable is precisely what is observed when those with phobias learn to conquer their fears. Rather than learning to "not fear" whatever it is that they fear—a nasty spider, for example— they instead learn not to let that fear paralyze them or make them cower in retreat. Thus, the solution to fear is not getting rid of the fear; it is teaching bravery in the presence of that fear! This is what we all must exemplify. In summary, it takes courage to take perspective, but by valuing education, as I have repeated, it makes it easier to be courageous and take perspective.

Chapter VII

The Power of Play

"Play is foundational for bonding relationships and fostering tolerance. It's where we learn to trust and where we learn about the rules of the game. Play increases creativity and resilience, and it's all about the generation of diversity—diversity of interactions, diversity of behaviors, diversity of connections." (1)

-Isabel Behncke, Ethologist and Primatologist

....

I know what you might be thinking, and it would probably be the first thing out of all my friends' mouths, too. "What do you mean by 'play'?" This is an honest and worthwhile question. I will admit that it is a hard task to define play, especially in the context of adulthood. After all, play can be regarded as childish, immature, and out of place in an adult's world of serious attitudes and endeavors (2). Considering that the word "play" comes up only in the context of kids goofing around in an unserious, impractical manner, it is understandable for the reader to twist their neck and squint their eyebrows in confusion. However, in the words of contemporary British painter David Hockney, "People tend to forget that play is serious." (3)

When I say "play," I mean, more specifically, engaging in self-directed sports or recreation, actively engaging or taking part in a game, or frolicking with peers (4, 5). Still, even with this definition, the reader might be thinking that play is something that carries no benefit, has no practical feasibility, and is unnecessary beyond joyful pleasure and goof-around time. In truth, however, play is one of the most important things we can do, especially in the context of American political discourse and creating a unified country.

My reasoning? To answer that, first, it is important to remember the goal of this book: the problem I am setting out to help solve. The goal is to break down destructive "us/ them" behavior and motivate the complex social skills necessary for cooperation. In other words, the aim is to help get rid of the hate and animosity that seem to be plaguing those with different political views so that we can get all Americans to see each other as integral parts of one awesome team. Simply put, I aim to help unify those who have been disconnected through nature's destructive randomness.

Now, what is the answer to why play is essential, valuable, and downright practical? The quote at the beginning of this chapter beautifully encapsulates this. Play builds bonds with and tolerance of "them-s." Playing is all about creating relationships with others and practicing these complex social skills, such as perspective taking, individuation, and compromise skills. Play allows you to see the humanity in others; it nurtures commonalities. This is precisely how to break down "us/them-ing."

Creating New Relationships

As a recap, Chapter 5 was all about establishing a superordinate goal. Why? It creates a shared aim and uses such commonality as a way to break down "us/them-ing." It primes people to think of similarity rather than differences. In a sea of division, it allows people to practice striving toward the same pursuit, an underlying bond beneath all the polarity. Play serves a similar function because it creates new relationships. Games are all about cooperation and fitting in (6).

Let's take an example of elementary school children during a physical education (PE) class. Take the perspective of your 10-year-old self walking into gym class during the crisp hours of the morning on a Friday. Imagine the environment, the smell, the jitteriness of all the young animals, and the hope of being able to goof off and play a fun game instead of running the mile. You say to yourself, 'This is the last day of school for the week; I hope we have it easy today."

As you walk into class, to your fortunate surprise, the teacher tells the class that the activity of the day is dodgeball! Assuming you actually liked dodgeball as a child (and I acknowledge that some of the readers did not have this experience), this just made your day. However, instead of being teamed up with all your best buddies, you get put on a team with some kids you don't know very well or have a bad relationship with. You have been placed with a bunch of "them-s." At first, you feel uncomfortable being surrounded by people you think are so incredibly different from you that it is hard to believe you even must share a class with "them". These are all people you look down upon.

Yet, as soon as the game starts and the balls start flying overhead, whizzing by like artillery, there is a switch. No longer are these other kids on your team "them-s"; they are your teammates, and you start behaving with respect to that classification over any other. All the previous groups you associate your teammates with fall to the wayside, as they are less important at this moment. First and foremost, the only thing you begin to behave with respect to is how you and all your teammates can charge through battle and come out victorious.

As the game progresses, one by one, your teammates get knocked out. Out of nowhere, you get beamed from the side and now knocked out yourself. After a few minutes, it is now a 1v1, and the person you usually look down upon is the only person left on your team.[54] Even if you think to yourself, "It's all up to this loser?!', that thought is followed up with, "Well, I hope he clutches up." Now, more than ever, you are rooting for the kid you previously saw no connection with.

The game is a nail biter; you feel your heartbeat starting to race, and the nerves kick in. A miracle happens: he manages to catch a ball that was thrown directly at his chest, securing the victory for your team! Ecstatic with joy and surprise, you and your teammates jump up and triumphantly shout, and run over to the kid and celebrate the win. Imagine the smiles, the laughter, the thrill, and the happiness you feel for yourself and for your

---

[54] Even if one of your friends was the last person left on the other team, you would want nothing more than to rub it into your friend's face that they lost to your team. This is a moment-to-moment recategorization of "us" and "them."

teammates. For the short span of this dodgeball game, you are able to behave as if those "others" are not so bad after all. That is the power of play.

Play is all about creating new relationships that challenge previously existing stereotypes. After all, the more interactions with "them-s" you have, the more exceptions accumulate that challenge essentialist stereotyping. (7) Contact through play provides more opportunities for the stimulus that is the "other" to be paired with new events that conflict with the stimuli with which they have already been paired. Effectively, play conditions new responses in the context of "others." This is precisely why playing— getting together, hanging out, kicking back, grabbing a beer, smoking a cigarette or joint,[55] watching a sports game, eating a meal together, singing karaoke, going for a hike, throwing a frisbee, playing dodgeball—creates friendships. Shared experiences bond people.[56] If 'us/them-ing' is based on minimally shared characteristics, well, we need to create some shared experiences!

Let's go through quick exercise. Think of the political ideology that you oppose the most. Okay, got it? Now, think of what a person who espouses that ideology looks like. What color is their hair? Is it clean or dirty? Straight or curly? What facial features do they have? A large nose? Wide eyes? Any weird moles, disfigurements, amputations, or other abnormalities? How do they smell? Are they generally pretty or ugly? How intelligent are they?

---

[55] This one assumes that you are of age and live in a state where cannabis is legal.

[56] This is precisely why Fraternities require a devote and brutal pledging process for any new initiates.

Whatever your answers are, they are generalizations that you have been conditioned to establish as a stereotype. Be humble and recognize that.

Now, imagine that same terrible person is a fan of the same sports teams as you. Pretend that you are having a beer with them at one of their games. But that's not all: their favorite music artists turn out to be your favorite artists. Pretend, you see them at one of their concerts, dancing and partying the night away with no care for anything political. They may have similar childhood stories of breaking the same bone or having the same surgery as you had. Pretend to show each other similar scars and talk about how awful the pain was. They may have a similar, humiliating experience with medical issues, just as you have. Pretend that you have the same color inhaler or braces as each other. Their family lineage comes from the same countries as yours. Pretend you both tell each other the story of the first person in your family to seek a new life in America. They may have the same favorite TV shows and movies as you. Pretend laughing with them about your favorite episodes.

One by one, with each additional shared trait or behavior, this person starts to lose the darkness you have painted on them with your previous generalization. You begin to paint a new, less offensive, more realistic picture of "them." A picture that is not as ghoulish, stinky, racist, ugly, foolish, and all that you find repulsive. Something more tolerable, relatable, and even likable. At this point, with the cognitive dissonance that might be flustering the reader, it might even be hard to envision this stereotypical representation of your political nemesis. Or, at least, you still picture the same stereotype, but this time, with a little touch of humanity and commonality. This is done because the reader is individuating instead of overgeneralizing. They are behaving with respect to the person as an individual rather than part of a foreign group. Successful cultures thrive on cooperation, compromise, and play. We can work our hearts out to learn all the contingencies that have affected the lives and behaviors of others, and we will never be able to do so. No amount of dialogue will perfectly encapsulate their repertoire. Don't get me wrong: we can learn a tremendous amount of information from letting others talk, and we must talk to others about our differences. However, we can do something additional to help mediate that pursuit. Along with talking through differences, we must create similarities with "thems" direct and intimate social bonds over fun things unrelated to politics.

Play as Practice

As a recap, Chapter 6 was all about perspective taking, listening to and tolerating the views of others, and the courage to compromise. Why? Because even after establishing a superordinate goal (fulfilling the Preamble), we will still disagree on how to best achieve that goal. After all, this is what we would expect, with everyone being unique. Exercising these complex social skills allows us to effectively talk through our inevitable differences without ripping each other's heads off or disowning family or friends, helping bring us one step closer to the ideal unified country we all want to enjoy. Play allows us to practice these skills. Learning how to interact with others, compromise, regulate emotions, and work together all occur when playing. (8, 9)

Play is more than a fun way to create new relationships between people and select more inclusive "us" behavior. Play is also a fun way to better ourselves and everyone we play with. When playing, not only are you practicing these social skills, but so is whoever you are playing with. It's a double whammy! Play is mutually beneficial. It is no wonder that play has been selected to be intrinsically reinforcing (fun in and of itself); it has extraordinary developmental benefits for everyone, both children and adults. (10, 11)

Perspective taking, individuating, and conversation and compromise skills, just like other behaviors, all require much practice. In the same way that a basketball player builds skill by shooting tens of thousands of free throws, we must put in the repetitions to develop our social skills. After all, we can only expect to get good at something if we practice, so we must practice. And if we stop putting in the hours, it should not be a shock when our skills fall short of our hopes.

For instance, if you never practice staying calm when listening to opinions that upset you, it could be a real struggle to stay calm when you run into someone with a drastically different point of view than you. Imagine you are very "pro-x," and someone who is very "anti-x" voices their opinions to you in all their uncensored honesty. Without having former practice staying calm in the face of upsetting ideas, you may be likelier to lash out and become aggressively defensive, segregating that person as a nasty "them." However, with some practice, almost anything is possible—even tolerating those you find most upsetting and misguided politically.

As the reader, you may still feel a little wishy-washy about how, exactly, play can prepare for something such as perspective taking. So, here is an example to demonstrate how exactly (social) play trains such social skills.[57]

Imagine getting home just in time to sit out on the porch and watch the sunset's symphony of colors ignite the sky—a perfect conclusion to your exhausting day. You see your neighbor already sitting outside, awaiting the splendid finale, and he asks if you would care to join him.[58] Excited to talk with your friendly neighbor, you agree and go over to his porch.[59] You both spend the next 30 beautiful minutes gazing out at the horizon and go back and forth telling funny stories to get a good knee slap out of the other. From childhood traumas to workplace nuisances, memories spill out, filling the air with warm laughter.

Every time you tell a story, your neighbor is actively taking the perspective of the version of

---

[57] Any kind of play that involves two or more people is regarded as social play. Social play is how we learn to compromise, negotiate, recognize one another's needs, and please one another. (12)

[58] This quest to enjoy the sunset together could possibly be thought of as the superordinate goal. So, right off the bat, you both at least have one commonality and motivation to break down any divisive "us/them-ing."

[59] Here, I would like to get into the idea of sharing a drink or smoking with the neighbor, but I recognize that not every reader partakes in these recreations. Yet this would be a perfect opportunity to share such things and bond over the common use of whichever drug of choice you consume. Establishing similar contingencies (behaviors), as we know, creates new relationships and helps break down destructive "us/them" behavior.

yourself in that story. Every time they tell a story, you are actively taking the perspective of the person in their story.[60] Just from sitting back and telling funny stories, you are both practicing perspective taking skills. Subsequently, while pretending to be the person in the other's story of childhood embarrassment or workplace disaster, you both become aware of the emotions brewing in the body of the other. You engage with those manipulative foreign feelings, get rattled with empathy, and then return to reality. Doing so involves practicing emotional regulation as well. Through story after story, you catch a glimpse of your neighbor's past experiences and start to piece together why they are the interesting individual they are. This is practicing individuation.

And there you have it: a simple example of how social play as an adult can train multiple essential social skills that facilitate cooperation and break down "us/them-ing."

Finding New Playmates

Here is a key point to consider. Across species, the bigger the average size of the social group, (a) the larger the brain, relative to total body size, and (b) the larger the neocortex, relative to total brain size. First shown in birds and primates by British anthropologist Robin Dunbar, there is a link between an increase in social complexity and the evolutionary expansion of the neocortex (the "newest" parts of the brain, evolutionarily speaking). From an RB perspective, this makes perfect sense. As the size of your group gets bigger,

---

[60] Highlighting social play has communal benefits.

there will be more people in your social network, providing more opportunities to practice complex social skills, resulting in an enlarged area of the parts of the brain that are involved in such behavior. This point was reiterated in a neuroimaging study of captive macaque monkeys housed in different-sized groups. This study showed that even on the scale of an individual monkey's lifetime, a larger group meant more thickening of the prefrontal cortex and other brain regions involved in theory of mind activities (such as perspective taking). This being so with other primates, this link is also observed in humans. The larger the size of someone's social network (as measured by e-mail/text relationships), the larger the vmPFC, and the better the person is at theory of mind-related skills, such as perspective taking. (13, 14, 15, 16)

Thus, play is great, and I hope I have made that clear, but what we should really be focusing on is playing, specifically with many different and new people. The reason, as I just pointed out with the neuroimaging studies, is that the more we can expand our social network, the more opportunities there will be to practice our social skills, and the better we will become at cooperating in larger group settings. Furthermore, the more we practice across different settings (different people), the more our social skills will generalize or unfold in many contexts. Basically, by practicing with many new and diverse people, you will be in a better position to apply those social skills to more new people.

Therefore, we all must take it upon ourselves to find new people to play with. The government cannot regulate that we talk to new people; it cannot be written into law that you must go out and meet someone every week or pay a fine of $500. It is our individual responsibility, and it takes courage.

Now, bear with me, this may be hard at first, and maybe even a little frightening, but that challenge is exactly why we must do it. We must train our courage and practice doing the right thing, even when it is the harder thing. If we hope to be courageous in the future, we must practice being courageous now. This little caveat is the knockout punch to put "us/ them-ing" to sleep and the crème de la crème for making these social skills fluent in your repertoire.

Remember, social play is mutually beneficial. Thus, making new relationships with "them-s" is something every reader can go out and do, today, to make the world a better place. As we have all heard before, you should be the change you want to see in the world. If you dream of a world where people can put down their guns, stop fighting, and all be friends, that starts with you. If you dream of a world where people can get along, regardless of their beliefs, that starts with you. If you dream of a world where people will be judged based on the content of their character and not some stereotype, that starts with you. **You** must reach out to those you think you are in conflict with and have a meal together to talk everything through. **You** must be willing to sit down and peaceably have a conversation with even the most disgusting of "them-s." After all, how else are you ever going to understand "them," and how are they ever going to understand you? There will never be a middle ground if we never sit down and find it; that which is not looked for will not be seen. **You** must take perspective, **you** must individuate, and **you** must tolerate and appreciate unique perspectives. **You** must be courageous. We all must take on the responsibility of exposing ourselves to a diverse set of people and expanding our social networks. [61] This is the best thing any one person can do to stop the hate, the "us/theming," the disgust, the frowning-upon, the resentment, the bitterness towards others. This is how we can all achieve the goals stated in the Preamble; this is how we unify as a country.

The impact of getting together with "them-s" involves no exaggeration. Even between people in the most opposite camps, getting together, talking, and sharing a meal can be the best way to start planting the seeds in the relationship so that cooperation can flourish. This next chapter is a testament to this—a motivating story of optimism that shows it is possible to bridge the gap between even the most divided. It is a story to model our own behavior after.

---

[61] This is why it has been my goal to show the reader the importance of owning up to and fulfilling this responsibility, providing a motivation for such prosocial behavior.

Chapter XIII

The Story of Daryl Davis

"If you want to solve this problem of racism, we need to stop focusing on the symptoms. Don't worry about the fear, don't worry about the hatred, those are just symptoms. That's like putting a Band-Aid on cancer, you gotta go down to the bone and treat it at its source. The source of all of this, is ignorance. Ignorance can be cured. The cure for ignorance is called education. So, you fix the ignorance? There's nothing left to fear... If there's nothing to fear, there's nothing to hate. If there's nothing to hate, there's nothing to destroy. So we need to focus on the ignorance, and we address it with exposure and education and conversation. We spend way too much time in this country talking about the other person, talking at the other person, talking past the other person. And why not just spend a little bit of time talking with the other person?"

- Daryl Davis (1)

....

With a father in the US foreign services, Daryl spent his early childhood bouncing back and forth from the United States to wherever in the world his dad was stationed. When he was overseas, he would go to elementary school with kids from all over the world. They came from Nigeria, Italy, France, Germany, Japan, Russia, you name it; if a country had an embassy in the city he was in, he went to school with children from that country. And he got along fine with all the other children. Regardless of where they were from or what they looked like, they all played together. Daryl developed a history of interacting, playing, and being friends with all people of many different appearances. Thus, growing up, he did not learn to be racist or judge someone based on the color of their skin but rather on the content of their character, thus living Dr. Kings dream. He did not know what racism was.

It was not until a Cub Scout parade at the age of 10 that he experienced his first bout with racism. He and his scout troop were marching from Lexington, Virginia, to Concord, Massachusetts to commemorate the ride of Paul Revere. Daryl, the only Black person in the whole scout troop and possibly the whole parade itself, carried the American flag and led his scout troops. Along the sidewalks were people cheering, waving American flags, and playfully shouting, 'The British are coming!' For the most part, the atmosphere was positive and filled with patriotic ecstasy. However, there was one small pocket of White adult men and children, maybe only five people in a sea of other White people, who were throwing rocks and bottles at Daryl.

At first, and this shows how naive Daryl was because of his overseas elementary school experience, he thought the people throwing the rocks and bottles simply did not like the scouts. It was not until his den mother and troop leaders huddled over him to protect him from all of the thrown debris and ushered him to safety that he realized that he was the only target, and nobody else was getting the same protection from the scout leaders—nobody else needed it. Daryl, in his heated confusion, kept asking his scout leaders if he had done something wrong. He was trying to figure out what he had done to make these people angry enough to try to hurt him. Still trying to get away from the danger, his scout leaders shushed him and never answered his question.

After the parade, when he got home, his parents asked how he fell to get all those scratches. He told his parents that he didn't fall and recounted the whole story about what, exactly, had happened. Then, for the first time in his life, his parents sat him down and told him what racism was. Racism is the belief that race is a fundamental determinant of human traits and capacities and that racial differences produce the inherent superiority of a particular race. (2) At the age of 10 in 1968, he had never heard the term "racism." This was beyond his comprehension. After all, the kids and adults who threw bottles and rocks at him looked no different than his French, German, Irish, Swedish, or fellow American friends, so he knew it had nothing to do with the skin color of the perpetrators. He thought his parents were lying to him.

He could not come to process the idea that someone who had never seen him or spoken to him, someone who knew nothing about him, could want to inflict pain upon him for no other reason than the color of his skin. Then, about a month and a half later, on April 4, Martin Luther King was assassinated. He remembers very vividly all the cities — Washington, DC, Chicago, Philadelphia, Detroit, Baltimore, Richmond, LA — that were burned to the ground. There was all this violence and destruction because of this new word he had just recently learned: racism. This made him realize that his parents were, in fact, telling the truth. Racism does indeed exist. But he was left asking, "Why?" Okay, it is real, but why? He came to the question, "How could someone hate me when they don't even know me?"

Instead of coming to hate those who hated him, he became genuinely curious about how they had come to learn their racist beliefs. He knew that it was nothing about how they were born, that it was not some evil residue of their soul responsible for their racism; racism is learned. With this realization, Daryl came to see the value of taking the perspectives even of those who have the most offensive beliefs. He was motivated to learn about others' perspectives. Instead of shying away from those appalling opinions, he did as much reading and research as he could about racism, reading especially into the history of the Ku Klux Klan.

Down the Road

Let's fast forward to Daryl's adult life. He became a musician with a degree specifically in jazz, but he can play anything: rock, blues, swing. He jokes, in all seriousness, that if someone was willing to pay to hear it, he was willing to play it. One day on the road, he and the band he was with at the time were performing at a bar in Frederick, Maryland, and once again, just like at his Cub Scout parade, he was the only Black person in the bar. This was an all-White bar, meaning that, though Black people could go in, they chose not to go in; they were not welcomed there.

Upon finishing the first set, while walking up to the table reserved for the band, someone put their arm around his shoulder. It was a White man who just wanted to tell Daryl that he really liked all their music. This White man then pointed to the stage and said, "This is the first time I have ever heard a Black man play piano like Jerry Lee Lewis." Daryl was surprised more than offended because this White man seemed older than he was yet did not know the Black origin of Jerry Lee Lewis' style of piano playing. So, Daryl explained, he got his style from the same place Lewis got his style, from Black blues and boogie-woogie artists. The White man was in disbelief, "No, no, no, Jerry Lee invented that. I ain't never heard no black man play like that, except for you." Daryl continued to explain how he actually knew Jerry Lee Lewis and he had told him where he had learned his style of playing, but the White man did not believe he knew Lewis, or that Lewis had learned anything from a Black person.

Still, the man asked to buy him a drink, fascinated by Daryl, as if he were a novelty. Daryl agreed, sat down, and had a cranberry juice, and it was then that the White man announced to Daryl, "This is the first time I've ever sat down and had a drink with a Black man." Now, Daryl is in disbelief. How can that be? So, innocently, Daryl asked him, why? After a few seconds of not answering, the White man's friend started egging him on: "Go on, tell him, tell him." The White man looked at Daryl square in the face and said, "I am a member of the Ku Klux Klan." At first, out of shock and thinking it was a joke, Daryl laughed. After all, since he was a child, Daryl had read books and studied the KKK.

There was no way a member of the KKK would come up, put their arm around a Black man and buy him a drink. So, the White man pulled out his Klan membership card. After recognizing the Klan's insignia, the white cross with the red blood drop in it, Daryl went cold. Still, they continued talking, and as they finished their drinks, Daryl asked some questions about the Klan and made light conversation.

As they were parting ways, the Klan member gave Daryl his phone number and told Daryl to let him know whenever he and his band came back to that bar to play. He wanted to bring all of his friends, Klan members, to see this Black guy play piano like Jerry Lee Lewis.[62] Daryl agreed and said, "I'll call you." Daryl called him about every six weeks to tell the Klan members that he was performing at this bar on such and such days. And the Klansman came and brought all the other Klan members. Now, these Klan members did not come to the bar in their robes and hoods; they came in street clothes.

On breaks, Daryl would go to the table of the White man who originally gave Daryl his number. Some members of the Klan, very curious about Daryl, would come up and talk to him, while others would shy away, stay back, and avoid him, just wanting to see him and not have to deal with him. Daryl was fine with both responses from the Klan members. Simply avoiding them sure beat the hell out of being attacked by them.

---

[62] When Daryl tells this story, he makes a joke right here and says, "I'm not sure he calls me 'a Black guy' to his friends, but…" He makes light of the fact that he knows these Klan members will be referring to him by the N-word.

About three or four months later, Daryl decided to write a book about the Klan, where he went around from state to state, interviewing different leaders of the KKK. When he published it, he became the first Black man to write a book about the KKK, which was written from the perspective of actually sitting down with leaders of the Klan for interviews. Though Black authors had written books about the Klan before, none had ever sat down with national heads of the Klan and had conducted interviews. Up to that point, only White authors had the safety to do such a thing. A White man could simply join the Klan as an undercover agent, quit, and then write about his experience.

So, what was his book about? It was an answer to the question posed when he was 10 years old: "How can you hate me when you don't even know me?" And who better to ask this question than someone who would take the time to join an organization whose whole premise for the past 100 years has been hating people who do not look like them and people who do not believe as they believe. Daryl thought to himself, "Someone who would go as far as to join the KKK should damn sure have an answer to this question." Thus, Daryl decided to get back in touch with this Klan member from the old bar to see whether he could help get in contact with the Grand Dragon (a state leader) of Maryland for his old chapter, Roger Kelly, for his first interview.[63]

---

[63] I say "old" because at this point, when Daryl contacted him again, he was no longer in the Klan. However, this was not because of a change of heart from talking with Daryl but rather because he was banished for something unrelated to Daryl.

At first, the man from the bar refused to give Kelly's phone number to Daryl. Not only would this old Klan member get in trouble for giving a Black man the information about the Grand Dragon, but he would not want to bring a Black man to the Grand Dragon of the largest KKK chapter in the state of Maryland. [64] He was concerned about both his and Daryl's safety. Yet, after some talking, Daryl convinced the man to give him Kelly's contact information, under the one condition that Daryl did not tell Kelly where he had gotten the information. Daryl obliged. However, before Daryl left to get in contact with Kelly, the man said, "Daryl, do not go to Roger Kelly's house, he will kill you." Roger Kelly was not someone to fool with.

Daryl took that advice, and instead of confronting Kelly at his house, Daryl gave his assistant, Mary (a White woman), Kelly's phone number to give him a call. Daryl told her to ask Kelly if he would be willing to sit down with "her boss" (Daryl), since he was writing a book about the Klan. However, Daryl made it clear to his assistant that she was not to tell him that her boss was Black. Daryl did not want Kelly to either turn the interview down or come prepared with different answers to the questions. Thus, Mary called Kelly, and he agreed to do the interview. They agreed to meet at a motel room above the local bar Kelly would always hang out at with his fellow Klan members.

---

[64] Daryl notes that, at this time, there were probably about 100 members in Roger Kelly's chapter, which was rather large for that time period.

The First Interview

The day came, and at the exact tick of the clock when the interview was to begin, there was a knock at the motel room door. Roger Kelly entered along with his bodyguard, who was decked out in camouflage, KKK merchandise, and a gun holstered on his hip. A Grand Dragon of the KKK meets Black jazz musician Daryl Davis; it seems like the most extreme 'us/them' dynamic in America.

When Roger Kelly and his bodyguard entered, Daryl stood up, showed that his hands were empty, walked over to Kelly, extended his right hand, and said, "Hi, Mr. Kelly, I'm Daryl Davis." Kelly shook his hand. No violence erupted, and the interview was off to a good start. Daryl then ushered them into the room, inviting them to have a seat. And they both sat down. Even better, it seemed as if Kelly was actually going to do the interview, even knowing that Daryl was Black.

Within 10 minutes of starting the interview, Kelly gave his answers as to why he would hate someone like Daryl— how he could hate a Black person simply for the color of their skin. Kelly went through the list of classical white supremacist beliefs: Black people are inferior, more prone to crime, and criminals, which is why there are more Black people in jail than White people; Black people are lazy and don't want to work, while they prefer to scam the government welfare system; Black people have smaller brains than White people, which is why their IQs are lower than those of White people. All these claims were, indeed, very offensive. However, Daryl didn't take offense. Instead, he said to himself, "Why should I be offended by someone who knows nothing about me?" Kelly had only seen the color of Daryl's skin and was making all kinds of overgeneralized assessments on that basis alone. Kelly only saw Daryl as Black, as a "them." Daryl again said to himself, "Why should I be offended by someone who is telling a lie?" With that "mindset under his belt," he could tolerate Kelly and sit patiently while he allowed Kelly to talk his heart out.[65] Daryl did not jump down Kelly's throat or become aggressively defensive. He let Kelly talk and give his full and honest perspective. Daryl was not there to fight Kelly; he was there to learn about his perspective.

This kind of tolerance, letting others utter their unfiltered opinions, even if those opinions could be considered deeply offensive and highly inaccurate, is the archetypal behavior I want all readers to come away from this book with and model their behavior after. Daryl developed the precise motivation and skillset I am trying to instill in all the readers with this book. Daryl knew that the KKK members were not tainted, that they had learned to be that way, and he wanted to learn why. He was motivated to expose himself to the perspectives of others.

All of these racist ideas were claims Daryl had heard before while doing his prior research into the Klan, so he was prepared for such responses. After Kelly was done speaking, Daryl went through Kelly's answers one by one and offered his insight as to why Kelly was wrong. Daryl told Kelly that he had never been convicted of any crime or been on welfare, and that he had not measured his brain, but he predicted it would be the same size as anybody else's. Still, as one would expect, Kelly

---

[65] "Mindset under his belt" is mentalistic, but it does bring some imagery to the page.

brushed it off, thinking whatever about it, not budging from his stance and reasons that Black people are inferior to White people.

Then, something pivotal in the interview happened. Out of nowhere, a noise startled Daryl, causing an observable panic and reflexive reaction. Daryl was 100% sure the suspicious noise came from Kelly, and in that split second of fear, Daryl got in the ready position to pounce from his chair and tackle Kelly and his bodyguard. During a time that could be measured by the snap of a finger, Daryl remembered the words of the old Klansman who had given him Kelly's number: "Daryl, do not fool with Kelly, he will kill you." Daryl went into fight mode. But thankfully, before there became any more commotion, Mary figured out what the noise was and calmly settled everyone down.

It turned out that Daryl was wrong. Kelly did not make the noise; in fact, Kelly was just as confused and shaken by the noise as Daryl. After getting the men to relax, Mary showed that the noise came from the soda cans shifting in the ice bucket they had prepared with soft drinks. It made sense. Before the start of the interview, Daryl, knowing that tensions were going to be hot, wanted to be able to offer up a cold beverage at the very least to be hospitable. When Kelly and his bodyguard first came in, Daryl offered them a drink, and they both declined, so they all forgot about it. After Mary explained the situation, the noise happened again, and they all began laughing at how foolish they all had been.

In that moment of relief, they all connected over how ignorant they had been. For that short moment, they all acted as an "us" to the tunes of their laughter. I guess, after all, the drinks really were an icebreaker. For the rest of the interview, the conversation and the tension loosened.

Connecting with Kelly

The conversation continued. They wrapped up, shook hands, and Kelly and his bodyguard said to keep in touch. It was a surprising thing to be told, as a Black man, by a leader of the KKK: "Keep in touch." However, per the request, Daryl kept in touch with Kelly, just like he did with the old Klansman who gave him Kelly's contact information. Daryl would call to tell Kelly that he was playing in the county and that he should come out and watch. Kelly actually came out to his gigs and watched!

Daryl then started inviting Kelly to come over to his house, and he came! He was accompanied by his bodyguard, but still, a leader of the KKK was going over to a Black man's house to have dinner. This was unbelievable! After some visits, the comfort level began to rise, and Daryl started inviting some of his Black friends, some Jewish friends, and some other White friends to meet and greet Kelly. This was meant just as a shock and exposure to Kelly but also a shock and exposure to his own friends as well. Even though some of his friends would freak out at first, they were all able to practice their social skills with an "other," all creating new relationships that challenged previously held stereotypes about the "other."

After two years had passed, Kelly would go over to Daryl's house without his bodyguard, by himself. This was an incredible sign of trust, and a huge step in their relationship. Yet, still, in those first two years of their relationship, Kelly never invited Daryl over to his house. It was not until

Kelly was promoted from Grand Dragon (state leader) to Imperial Wizard (national leader) that he started inviting Daryl over to his house. When Daryl would come over, Kelly would show him the Klan den, the room where they had Klan meetings, and talk about every little ritualistic detail.

At this point, Kelly started inviting Daryl to Klan rallies, where all Klan members wore their robes and hoods. This was the ceremony where Klan members circled a giant cross, lighting the base of the cross at the command of Kelly, give speeches talking about the future of the white race, and then eat hot dogs and hamburgers.[66] Daryl documented and took notes on all of it, and most of all, was allowed to eat the hot dogs and hamburger afterwards. He was breaking bread with even more "them-s."

At one of these Klan rallies, Kelly addressed his relationship with Daryl, saying, "I'd follow that

---

[66] In these speeches, members of the Klan would talk about various beliefs: the future of the White race, what the Constitution guarantees them, that this is a White man's land, this land was built by White people, the Constitution was signed by White men, this is their country, and other big topics or issues at the time. Now, I want to use this footnote to extend a previous footnote I added in Chapter 5, where I talked about the rebuttal to the idea that America is a country for White men. I will let the ideas of the KKK speak for themselves. Saying that America is a White man's land built by White people for White people is a White supremacist belief held by the Ku Klux Klan. Thus, to espouse the idea that America is only for White people is to repeat the exact same talking points as the KKK. Thus, to reaffirm my point in the footnote to Chapter 5, America is for everyone.

man to hell and back because I believe in what he stands for and he believes in what I stand for. We don't agree with everything, but at least he respects me to sit down and listen to me, and I respect him to sit down and listen to him." This was astonishing. Never did Daryl think that a leader, not just an ordinary member, of the KKK would show such admiration for a Black man.

Their relationship became one of true friendship. In the words of social development research professor Carrollee Howes of UCLA, "Friendships appear to facilitate conflict resolution and conflict avoidance." (3) This story is the perfect anecdote for this quote. Day by day, they gradually began to see each other as "us." In other words, the new relationship they were forming was dissolving this previously conditioned "us/them" barrier. Finally, after 6–7 years of friendship with Daryl, Kelly quit the Klan and gave Daryl his old robes because he no longer believed in what the Klan stood for.

Daryl repeated this method over and over again. As a result, he has directly and indirectly helped over 200 members of the KKK drop their robes and change their beliefs. (4, 5) Simply by having the courage to sit down, tolerate, take perspective, and create new relationships with his "adversaries," he has been able to change their perspectives and make "them" behave as "us."

Being Misunderstood

Although Daryl is working to mend the divide in America, his vision is not well received by some people, and his efforts are misunderstood by many. However, I can understand the confusion; after all, not everyone has heard the full story as I have just laid it out. Seeing a black man stand next to KKK members probably spins the heads of people unaware of Daryl's mission to answer the question he formed at the age of 10: "How can you hate me, when you don't even know me?"[67]

Daryl will catch flak for defending the KKK's freedom of speech and right to peacefully assemble. For example, while at a protest in Charlottesville, one woman shouted out at Daryl, "You're a person of color. Why are you talking to them?" Daryl responded, "That's right, I am a person of color, but I'm also an American and so is this man right here." (6) If this does not remind us of Chapter 5 and superordinate goals, I don't know what could! It does not matter what you believe, it does not matter what skin color you are, the insignificant differences do not matter; we are all America's with the ability to speak freely and the responsibility to allow others to do so.

If Daryl could make this work at the most extreme levels of hate, then we can make it work despite our slight levels of irritation over policy debates and social media drama. We must find our commonalities with others and then expand outward from those; as Daryl said, even the KKK like music. The method is to start with that one

---

[67] It is actually quite ironic. Daryl set out on a mission to find out how people could hate him without having met him, but then was faced with people (White and Black) who hated him without ever knowing him because of his efforts to get to know KKK members. Once again, this reaffirms what Daryl said after the Cub Scout incident: it was not about color. The people who hate Daryl for his effort to connect with members of the KKK learned to hate Daryl in the same way as members of the KKK: conditioning.

commonality, create that similarity, and then progress from there. In a sea of diversity, we must find where we overlap.

In Summary

Daryl does not have a preset genetic code that has made him pursue the path he has chosen, nor did any of the KKK members he befriended have evil souls that made them white supremacists. Both sets of behaviors stem from conditioning—behavioral selection by the environment. In recognition of that, Daryl did not hold any of the KKK members' racist ideas against them, nor did he take offense to their outlandish opinions and hateful rhetoric.[68] Instead, he came to recognize the value of listening to their opinions —not censoring and ignoring but engaging with respectful conversation, forever motivated to take others' perspectives. Daryl is the exemplar every reader should model their behavior after.

There are many takeaways from his story, but the one I want to leave the reader with is this: don't set out to change people, set out to make them think. Setting out to change people or "convert" them into thinking the way you do completely ignores everything I have been trying to get across with this book. The goal is not to make others think as you do; this would be as ignorant as the aggressively intolerant man from my first rendition of the parable of the blind men and the elephant in Chapter 6. Rather, the goal is to get everyone to learn, question, be humble and honest, have

---

[68] Daryl embodies the phrase, 'Sticks and stones can break my bones, but words will never hurt me."

intellectual humility, put their own ideas on the chopping block, and remain open to criticism. Most importantly, we must think together as an "us."

Take Action!

We must remember that we are on the same team. We are together in this. As the Preamble to the Constitution says, "We, the People" — not just White or Black, straight or gay, man or women, rich or poor, but everybody. If you are not doing so already, start looking at your fellow American as a teammate, a collaborator, a part of the same great family that share the same powerfully liberating value that is individual liberty. Finally, forever remember this: whenever and wherever possible, find similarities with others, take their perspective, and play. This, in line with the values of education and courage, will bring us all closer to the idealistic future we dreamed of as children.

One Last Thought

The problem I stated in the introduction of this book concerned the growing minority of people who have not learned to tolerate others and take others' perspectives. I recognize that this is the target audience I need to reach the most but that will naturally be the hardest to reach. After all, not everyone will relinquish their old beliefs; some are as gung-ho as they come. Even with Daryl Davis, there were KKK members he met who would never in a million years change from their beliefs, and so are there those who will never be tolerant of other politics. There will always be a minority that will not change, no matter what.

So, what should you do with someone who is intolerant of you? The best thing you can do: set a good example and model correct behavior. In other words, be like Daryl. I cannot think of a better example of what to do when someone is intolerant. If you really cannot stand being around them and trying to play, then don't. Let them be. You don't have to be perfect; you just have to have the courage to not hold their beliefs against them.

So, to help get this message to those who need it most, I ask you to please recommend or send a copy of this book to a those who might need to hear it. If you found any resolve from this book, then hopefully, so will they. If I did my job correctly, I have provided an environment to motivate every reader to start choosing to be like Daryl and behave as "us."

Acknowledgments

I want to take this time to thank everyone who helped me during the writing process. Thank you, Mom and Dad, for always telling me I can do what I put my mind to. It was in large part through that motivating lesson of encouragement from a young age that I was conceived I could write this book. You have both been supportive in every way possible.

I also want to thank all of my friends and family who spent tireless hours in conversation about the ideas that were racing through my head during this process. Lydia, Ryan, Eric, Cole, and Philip, you all helped me challenge myself, better articulate my speech, and better hone in on the message I am trying to get across. Though not all of the conversations were necessarily fun, and there would be times where the daily calls to talk about the same subject could get repetitive or annoying, you all really stuck it out and were able to make the discussion worth the while.

References

Chapter 1 - The Old Philosophy

1. Meyer, P. J. *Mistakes Are Merely Steps up the Ladder.* Quotemaster. https://www.quotemaster.org/q0741c9835336b9 17fde0fd0195b9cd2e.
2. Kantor, J. R. *The Scientific Evolution of Psychology.* Principia Press, 1963, vol. 1, p. 117.
3. Gazzaniga, M. S. *The Consciousness Instinct: Unraveling the Mystery of How the Brain Makes the Mind.* Farrar, Straus, and Giroux, 2019, p. 17.
4. Singer, P. N. "Galen." *Stanford Encyclopedia of Philosophy*, Stanford University, 18 Mar. 2016,
5. Gazzaniga, M. S. *The Consciousness Instinct: Unraveling the Mystery of How the Brain Makes the Mind.* Farrar, Straus, and Giroux, 2019, p. 23.
6. Ibid., pp. 26–27.
7. Ibid., p. 31.
8. Ibid., p. 36.
9. Sapolsky, R. M. *Behave: The Biology of Humans at Our Best and Worst.* New York, NY, Penguin Books, 2018, p. 50.
10. Ibid., p. 8.
11. Watson, J. *Behaviorism,* 2nd ed. Norton, 1930.
12. Hume, D. *An Enquiry Concerning Human Understanding* (1784), in Hutchins, Adler, and Brockway, eds., *Great Books of the Western World,* vol. 35, *Locke/Berkeley/Hume,* Oxford University Press, p. 458.

13. Darwin, C. *The Descent of Man and Selection in Relation to Sex*, in Hutchins, Adler, and Brockway, *Great Books of the Western World,* vol. 49, *Darwin*, p. 319.

14. Rehman, I. "Classical Conditioning." *StatPearls [Internet]*, U.S. National Library of Medicine, 27 Aug. 2020. www.ncbi.nlm.nih.gov/books/NBK470326/.

15. "Freud." *Internet Encyclopedia of Philosophy.* https:// iep.utm.edu/freud/.

16. Skinner, B. F. *Science and Human Behavior.* Free Press, 1953, p. 357.

Chapter 2 - The New Philosophy

1. Skinner, B. F. *Science and Human Behavior.* Free Press, 1953, p. 5.

2. Skinner, B. F. *About Behaviorism.* New York, Random House, p. 3.

3. Ibid., pp. 37–50.

4. Sapolsky, R. M. *Behave: The Biology of Humans at Our Best and Worst.* New York, NY, Penguin Books, 2018, pp. 100–102.

5. Ibid., p. 102.

6. Ibid., pp. 103–104.

7. Skinner, B. F. *Science and Human Behavior.* Free Press, 1953, pp. 116, 139.

Chapter 3 - Selecting Behavior

1. Hayes, S. *A Liberated Mind.* Avery Publishing. 2020, p. 79.

2. Skinner, B. F. *About Behaviorism*. New York, Random House, p. 51.

3. American Psychological Association. "Antecedent." APA Dictionary of Psychology. https:// dictionary.apa.org/antecedent.

4. American Psychological Association. "Behavior." APA Dictionary of Psychology. https://dictionary.apa.org/ behavior.

5. Healtheworld. "The ABCs of Behavior Analysis!" *Heal the World Behavioral Services*. http:// www.healtheworld.net/uncategorized/the-abcs-ofbehavior-analysis/.

6. American Psychological Association. "Reinforcer." APA Dictionary of Psychology. https:// dictionary.apa.org/reinforcer.

7. American Psychological Association. "Reinforcement." APA Dictionary of Psychology. https://dictionary.apa.org/reinforcement.

8. American Psychological Association. "Punishment." APA Dictionary of Psychology. https:// dictionary.apa.org/punishment.

9. American Psychological Association. "Motivation." APA Dictionary of Psychology. https:// dictionary.apa.org/motivation.

10. American Psychological Association. "Establishing operation." APA Dictionary of Psychology. https:// dictionary.apa.org/establishing-operation.

11. Applied Behavior Analysis. "Motivating Operations."

http://abaappliedbehavioranalysis.weebly.com/
motivating-operations.html.

12. Serena, K. "Aron Ralston's Arm was Stuck under an 800-Pound Boulder. so He Amputated it to Survive." *All That's Interesting*, 26 Oct. 2021. https:// allthatsinteresting.com/aron-ralston-127-hours-truestory.

13. Lattal, K. A. (2012) Schedules of Reinforcement. In: Seel, N. M. (ed.), *Encyclopedia of the Sciences of Learning*. Boston, MA, Springer. P. 2929-2933. https:// doi.org/10.1007/978-1-4419-1428-6_990

14. Lumen. "Introduction to Psychology." https://courses.lumenlearning.com/wmopen-psychology/chapter/reading-reinforcement-schedules/.

Chapter 4 - Free Will

1. Jung, C. G. *Man and His Symbols*. Dell Publishing, 1964, p. 72.

2. American Psychological Association. "Free will." APA Dictionary of Psychology. https:// dictionary.apa.org/free-will.

3. Pierce, D. W. and Cheney, C. D. *Behavior Analysis and Learning*. Psychology Press, 2013, pp. 674–675.

4. American Psychological Association. "Matching law." APA Dictionary of Psychology. https:// dictionary.apa.org/matching-law.

5. American Psychological Association. "Bias." APA Dictionary of Psychology. https://dictionary.apa.org/ bias.
6. Baum, W. M. "On Two Types of Deviation from the Matching Law: Bias and Undermatching." *Journal of the Experimental Analysis of Behavior*, vol. 22, no. 1, 1974, pp. 231–242. https://doi.org/10.1901/ jeab.1974.22-231.
7. Sapolsky, R. M. *Behave: The Biology of Humans at Our Best and Worst*. New York, NY, Penguin Books, 2018, p. 609.
8. Stabel, A., et al. "Differential Reinforcement." *Encyclopedia of Autism Spectrum Disorders*, 2013, pp. 952–954. https://doi.org/10.1007/978-1-4419-1698-3_1902.

Chapter 5 - Our Shared Goals

1. Citycorp/Citybank and the Commission of the Bicentennial of the United States Constitution. *The Constitution of the United States, Official Commemorative Edition*. 1987.
2. Ito, T. and Urland, G. J. "Race and Gender on the Brain: Electrocortical Measures of Attention to the Race and Gender of Multiply Categorizable Individuals." *JPAP 85*, 2003, p. 616.
3. Sapolsky, R. M. *Behave: The Biology of Humans at Our Best and Worst*, New York, NY, Penguin Books, 2018, p. 420.
4. National Constitution Center. "The Preamble of the U.S.

Constitution."constitutioncenter.org/interactivec onstitution/preamble.

5. Gelman, A. *Red State, Blue State, Rich State, Poor State: Why Americans Vote the Way They Do*. Princeton University Press, 2010, p. 127.

Chapter 6 - Our Individual Goals

1. Sapolsky, R. M. *Behave: The Biology of Humans at Our Best and Worst*. New York, NY, Penguin Books, 2018, pp. 423–424.
2. Ibid., p. 422.
3. American Psychological Association. "Perspective taking." APA Dictionary of Psychology. https:// dictionary.apa.org/perspective taking.
4. Hiser, J. and Koenigs, M. "The Multifaceted Role of the Ventromedial Prefrontal Cortex in Emotion, Decision Making, Social Cognition, and Psychopathology." *Biological Psychiatry*, vol. 83, no. 8, 2018, pp. 638–647. https://doi.org/10.1016/ j.biopsych.2017.10.030.
5. Sapolsky, R. M. *Behave: The Biology of Humans at Our Best and Worst*. New York, NY, Penguin Books, 2018, p. 63.
6. Hiser, J. and Koenigs, M. "The Multifaceted Role of the Ventromedial Prefrontal Cortex in Emotion, Decision Making, Social Cognition, and Psychopathology." *Biological Psychiatry*, vol. 83, no. 8, 2018, pp. 638–647. https://doi.org/10.1016/ j.biopsych.2017.10.030.

7. Goldstein, B. E. (2010). *Encyclopedia of Perception*. SAGE Publications, p. 492.
8. University of Minnesota. *All Amendments to the United States Constitution.* http://hrlibrary.umn.edu/education/all_amendments_usconst.htm. "Liberalism English
9. Lexico Dictionaries. *Liberalism: Definition and Meaning.* https://www.lexico.com/en/definition/liberalism.
10. National Archives and Records Administration. *Declaration of Independence: A Transcription.* https://www.archives.gov/founding-docs/declarationtranscript.

Chapter 7 - The Power of Play

1. Quote Investigator. "You Can Discover More about a Person in an Hour of Play than in a Year of Conversation." 20 Nov. 2021. https://quoteinvestigator.com/2015/07/30/hour-play/.
2. Abrams, E. and Blazina, C. *Clinician's Guide to Treating Companion Animal Issues: Addressing Human-Animal Interaction.* London, United Kingdom, Academic Press, an Imprint of Elsevier, 2019, pp. 223–252.
3. The Strong National Museum of Play. "Play Quotes." 8 Nov. 2021. https://www.museumofplay.org/about/play-quotes/.
4. Merriam-Webster. "Play: Definition & Meaning." https://www.merriam-

webster.com/dictionary/play. 5.   Gray,   P. "What Exactly is Play, and Why is it Such a Powerful Vehicle for Learning?" *Topics in Language Disorders,* vol. 37, no. 3, 2017, pp. 217–228. DOI: 10.1097/TLD.0000000000000130.

6. Sapolsky, R. M. *Behave: The Biology of Humans at Our Best and Worst.* New York, NY, Penguin Books, 2018, p. 206.

7. Sapolsky, R. M. *Behave: The Biology of Humans at Our Best and Worst.* New York, NY, Penguin Books, 2018, p. 399.

8. Whitman, E. "The Impact of Social Play on Young Children." *Integrated Studies,* vol. 94, 2018.   https:// digitalcommons.murraystate.edu/bis437/94

9. Encourage Play. "Play and Social Skills." https:// www.encourageplay.com/open-ended-play.

10. Gray, Peter. *Play-Based Learning with Dr. Peter Gray.*   YouTube. https://www.youtube.com/watch?v=wJaAegok8 L4.

11. Bateson, P. "Play, Playfulness, Creativity and Innovation." *Animal Behavior and Cognition,* vol. 1, 2014, pp. 99–112.

12. Gray, P. "What Exactly is Play, and Why is it Such a Powerful Vehicle for Learning?" *Topics in Language Disorders,* vol. 37, no. 3, 2017, pp. 217–228. DOI: 10.1097/TLD.0000000000000130.

13. Sapolsky, R. M. *Behave: The Biology of Humans at Our Best and Worst*, New York, NY, Penguin Books, 2018, p. 429.

14. Dunbar, R.I. and Schultz, S. "Evolution in the Social Brain." *Sci*, vol. 317, 2007, p. 1344; Dunbar, R. I. "The Social Brain Hypothesis and its Implications for Social Evolution." *Ann Hum Biol*, vol. 36, 2009, p. 562; Pérez-Barbería, F. J., et al. "Evidence for Coevolution of Sociality and Relative Brain Size in Three Orders of Mammals." *Evolution*, vol. 61, 2007, p. 2811; Powell, J., et al. "Orbital Prefrontal Cortex Volume Predicts Social Network Size: An Imaging Study of Individual Differences in Humans." *Proc Royal Soc B: Biol Sci* 2012, p. 2157; Lewis, P. A., et al. "Ventromedial Prefrontal Volume Predicts Understanding of Others and Social Network Size." *Neuroimage*, vol. 57, 2011, p. 1624; Powell, J. L., et al. "Orbital Prefrontal Cortex Volume Correlates with Social Cognitive Competence." *Neuropsychologia*, vol. 48, 2010, p. 3554; Lehmann, J. and Dunbar, R. I. "Network Cohesion, Group Size and Neocortex Size in Female-Bonded Old World Primates." *Proc Royal Soc B: Bio Sci*, vol. 276, 2009, p. 4417; Sallet, J., et al. "Social Network Size Affects Neural Circuits in Macaques." *Sci*, vol. 334, 2011, p. 697.

15. Sapolsky, R. M. *Behave: The Biology of Humans at Our Best and Worst*. New York, NY, Penguin Books, 2018, p. 430.

16. Powell, J., et al., "Orbital Prefrontal Cortex Volume Predicts Social Network Size: An Imaging Study of Individual Differences in Humans." *Proc Royal Soc B: Biol Sci*, vol. 279, 2012, p. 2157; Lewis, P. A., et al. "Ventromedial Prefrontal Volume Predicts Understanding of Others and Social Network Size." *Neuroimage*, vol. 57, 2011, p. 1624; Powell, J. L., et al. "Orbital Prefrontal Cortex Volume Correlates with Social Cognitive Competence." *Neuropsychologia*, vol. 48, 2010, p. 3554; Bickart, K. C., et al. "Amygdala Volume and Social Network Size in Humans." *Nature Neuroscience*, vol. 14, 2011, p. 163; Kanai, R., et al. "Online Social Network Size is Reflected in Human Brain Structure," *Proc Royal Soc B: Biol Sci*, vol. 279, 2012, p. 1327.

Chapter 8 - The Story of Daryl Davis

1. Rogan, J. "#1419 - Daryl Davis." Spotify, 30 Jan. 2020.https://open.spotify.com/episode/2iuVjCu9 yWOAxW87hUZT0U?si=1GpxMKr6Tfqx422rr oDRUQ.

2. Merriam-Webster. "Racism: Definition & Meaning." https://www.merriam-webster.com/dictionary/ racism.

3. Howes, C. "Friends and Peers." *Encyclopedia of Infant and Early Childhood Development*, 2008, Vol. 2. pp. 552–562. https://doi.org/10.1016/ b978-012370877-9.00066-9.

4. Davis, D. "Why I, as a Black Man, Attend KKK Rallies: Daryl Davis: TEDx Naperville." TED Talk. https://www.ted.com/talks/daryl_davis_why_i_a s_a_black_man_attend_kkk_rallies

5. Rogan, J. "#1419 - Daryl Davis." Spotify, 30 Jan. 2020.https://open.spotify.com/episode/2iuVjCu9 yWOAxW87hUZT0U?si=1GpxMKr6Tfqx422rr oDRUQ.

6. Simon, M. and Sidner, S. "When a Klansman Met a Black Man in Charlottesville." CNN, 16 July 2020. https://www.cnn.com/2017/12/15/us/ charlottesville-klansman-black-man-meeting/ index.html.

www.ingramcontent.com/pod-product-compliance
Lightning Source LLC
Chambersburg PA
CBHW060232030426
42335CB00014B/1419